# A Three-Ply Cord

## Making and Keeping Covenant Marriage

Written, Compiled, and Edited by

John Louis

The contents of this work, including, but not limited to, the accuracy of events, people, and places depicted; opinions expressed; permission to use previously published materials included; and any advice given or actions advocated are solely the responsibility of the author, who assumes all liability for said work and indemnifies the publisher against any claims stemming from publication of the work.

All Rights Reserved
Copyright © 2024 by John Louis

No part of this book may be reproduced or transmitted, downloaded, distributed, reverse engineered, or stored in or introduced into any information storage and retrieval system, in any form or by any means, including photocopying and recording, whether electronic or mechanical, now known or hereinafter invented without permission in writing from the publisher.

Dorrance Publishing Co
585 Alpha Drive
Suite 103
Pittsburgh, PA 15238
Visit our website at *www.dorrancebookstore.com*

ISBN: 979-8-89211-417-2
eISBN: 979-8-89211-832-3

# Table of Contents

Foreword . . . . . . . . . . . . . . . . . . . . . . . . . . . . . . . . . . .v
Front Notes . . . . . . . . . . . . . . . . . . . . . . . . . . . . . . . .ix
Guideposts . . . . . . . . . . . . . . . . . . . . . . . . . . . . . . . . . .1
Concepts of Covenant . . . . . . . . . . . . . . . . . . . . . . . . .19
Speaking – the Divine Gift of Creation . . . . . . . . . . . . .61
Healing the Wounds of the Embodied Spirit . . . . . . . .105
Gospel Scriptures Introduction . . . . . . . . . . . . . . . . . .129
Commentary on the Wedding Mass . . . . . . . . . . . . . . .161
Epilogue . . . . . . . . . . . . . . . . . . . . . . . . . . . . . . . . . .171

## Author's Foreword

"The aim of this instruction is love from a pure heart, a good conscience, and a sincere faith"(1Tim 1:5) and to "...set an example for those who believe, in speech, conduct, love, faith, and purity"(1Tim 4:12).

This book is not a novel nor a map. The first chapter presents the Judeo-Christian concept of 'being', that is, what it means to be a human created in the image and likeness of God. This is the foundation of all that follows in this work. It is from this point of understanding the remainder of any exploration should proceed. Any section or single scripture chosen after is at the inspiration of the Creator and the needs of the person engaging in the journey.

It is intended as a personal exercise and you are encouraged to use the purposed open spaces provided to record your own thoughts and record your inspirations. It becomes your prayerful work involving all of what the first chapter describes as your spiritual encounters, your works and actions of conscience, and your physical action in the written effort.

It is a journey intended for those who need to learn about marriage, those contemplating marriage, those who want to strengthen their marriage vows, and those who want to repair those covenant vows. Parents will find tools and understanding to help them instruct their children as "...all scripture is inspired by God and useful for teaching,..." This becomes especially important when parents find their children engaging in serious relationships. We are always parents, and perceived independence does not relieve us of our responsibilities in this area. Those engaging themselves in such relationships will find this work a useful tool in reviewing the foundation of the covenant relationship of Christian marriage, should they choose to make their marriage such a commitment. Parish catechists will find this collection based soundly on the scriptures and the Catechism of the Catholic Church. Quotations and references are provided in the text for broader exploration of the precepts the book is intending to promote.

The work of gathering the scriptures is born of the struggles to hold a marriage together. In this instance the work continues to be a successful daily exercise in commitment to the sacramental covenant marriage. It is for others seeking to do the same that the effort continued to bring this work to a public reality, available for the multiple purposes given above. The energy put into the effort is in empathy for all committed to marriage 'til death do us part'. Chapter four draws on the scriptures to provide hope and strengthen fortitude in the pursuit of this ideal. The virtue of Hope is extended to those who are at the beginning of their relationships so those involved in the joyfulness of the beginning of their lives may recognize together signs of difficulty and to be prepared to act when those signs emerge.

Grace and peace of God our Father, the blessing of our Lord, Jesus Christ, and the fellowship of the Holy Spirit be with you on your journey.

# Dedication

To my wife, Mindy, and for our family. For the adventures of a lifetime and the joy born of the trials, I thank you and I bless you.

*I am grateful for the personal and professional considerations given to this work by Dr. Maureen Groome for her efforts editing and her commentary on this work.*

# Front Notes

Scripture references are drawn from The Catholic Study Bible 3rd Edition, NABRE. Senior, Donald, John J. Collins, Mary Ann Getty Eds; New York, Oxford UP. 2010.Print.

Unless otherwise noted, definitions are from *Collins English Dictionary*. William Collins GenEd. New York; HarperCollins Publishing. www.dictionary.com LLC, 2020. On-line.

The patriarchal view of the scripture writing holds up the dignity of women as often as it infers the historical characterization as property. From Genesis, Man (hā'ādām) was created male (zākār) and female (n'qebāʰ) as partners. Other social factors of fallen humanity created inequities that continue to exist in societies worldwide. The scriptures are discussed here as applying to both male and female. Bias will perpetually be present by individual readers and evolving social contexts. The reader is encouraged to remember this while participating in the experience (translation resource Saint Pope John Paul II."*Man and Woman He Made Them*". Waldstein, M. Ed. p136, footnote 2).

Abbr. (CCC) - *Catechism of the Catholic Church. Second Ed*. Washington D.C., English Translation United States Catholic Conference. 1994. Print.

# GUIDEPOSTS

*Prayers to Begin*
"St. Michael the Archangel, defend us in battle. Be our defense against the wickedness and snares of the devil. May God rebuke him, we humbly pray, and do thou oh Prince of the heavenly hosts, by the power of God, thrust into hell Satan and all evil spirits who prowl about the world seeking the ruin of souls."

"Come, Holy Spirit. Fill the hearts of Thy faithful and enkindle in us the fire of Thy love. Send forth your spirit and we will be created, and You will renew the face of the earth."

**What Do You Believe?**
The boat dock at the restaurant was full of people on this warm Saturday night. A warm breeze was bringing in the sailboats and the power cruisers and smaller motorboats came and went regularly. The moon was shining full already as the sun's light faded from the opposite horizon. He knelt on one knee at the head of the pier and the crowd around them paused, taking time to witness the event. He presented her with a ring and said, "You make me want to be a better man. Would you join me through life's journey on our way to heaven? Marry me, please."

This was not how I proposed. It is how I wish I had proposed. But at a very young age of nineteen I had little understanding of the concept of marriage. I only knew that it wasn't an infatuation and that I had more to learn about love than I could imagine. These I learned from watching my parents, grandparents, aunts and uncles, and other married adults throughout my short years.

I did know she and I had a common understanding of the Christian faith. Our dates began with her asking a general question, "Do Catholics really believe…?" Answering that question took us through formal classes as well as Sundays attending each other's church community functions. We spent the Holy Week before Easter going from mass to mass and service to service. We witnessed baptisms and commitment rituals in both communities. Christianity was core to both our young lives.

What was your proposal experience? Did you get to plan the *romantic dinner*? Was it a complete surprise? Who proposed to whom? Am I stirring great memories, or scratching at an old wound? Either, or both, are intended. I *want* you to begin thinking about these events.

The question "What do you believe?" is core to a lasting marital commitment. Most often a couple will say they love each other. The question should be asked and answered how you love each other differently from anyone else you know and love. And, where do you intend this love will lead? The question of what one believes opens to all sorts of questions exploring the concept of love between a man and a woman. The question intends the couple learn the guiding principles of the other, the fundamentals of decision making, the invisible reality that guides the visible, tangible activity of the life of the other. What does happily ever after look like?

Sacramental marriage is a "…covenant between the spouses integrated into God's covenant with man: authentic married love is caught up into divine love." (CCC 1639) The union of the two persons with God as witness intends to create an unbreakable bond of conscience. "Where one alone may overcome, two together can resist. A three-ply cord not easily broken"(Eccl 4:12). The strength of the Sacrament of Marriage begins with common core principles of faith, of Catholic faith in this journey. The end is happily ever after in heaven with God.

Answering this question of common principles is the reason for this first chapter of our journey together. Let's continue to walk together and remember the foundations for our Christian community and the reasoning we use for knowing who and what we are and the tools we use to form our consciences.

## The Person, Formation of Conscience, and Guidelines for Free Will Choice

We must have a common idea of who and what we are as human beings before we begin our journey together. The Christian concept of personhood is muddled these past several decades in the rollover from one century to another, one millennium to the next. That God made us in His image is no longer the prevalent philosophy in Western society, nor is the mission He assigned us, to be fruitful and multiply and to care for this world. These two *Genesis mandates* are fundamental to the choices we make daily to meet the goals we plan for our lives. These need to be firm in our minds, that we may share a common purpose in a world where society promotes self-satisfaction without moral guidance or limitations.

Walk with me on a path of memory and recreation of the ideas that are fundamental Truths of humanity. The Way is counter-cultural, suggesting that we are more than the physical elements deciphered by science. We are more than just another animal species risen through evolution. There are reasons outside our senses for taking certain actions and refraining from others. Only when we act within given boundaries are we truly free to live a life worthy of our creation.

We are *embodied spirits*. We are body, mind/conscience, and spirit, created by God for the purpose of relationship with God. We are made of the 'stuff' of this world/universe, then enhanced by having life breathed into us by God, and given a free will to exercise our conscience. These three parts of our being are the parts that reflect the image of our Creator, no matter the language we speak or the color of our skin. These are the common denominators of humanity. The skills given each of us are the tools given to exercise the free-will of conscience, to act, and to work with each other towards the mission we have been given.

We are given to know the Creator God through the works of creation, nature's laws, and an instinctual comprehension of natural law, allowing us to comprehend a realization that there is more to our lives and our surroundings than what we see. There is an intangible understanding that certain actions are 'right' actions and certain actions are 'wrong' actions. We are given to seek the differences between these actions while seeking God who created us.

We seek out God with free will in that we have the freedom given by God to choose to be in relation with God or choose not to be in that relationship. This freedom of choice is exercised first in the mind where understanding is worked and developed. Next, we determine whether any given action we take after deciding is a virtue (right) or a vice (wrong). Our purpose is to develop our choices to make a habit of choosing virtue over vice, building our character in such a way as to build a relationship with God. The habit of making the 'right choice' leads to happiness and a sense of contentment of character that ultimately results in eternal life in a relationship with the Creator.

Concupiscence is the tendency of humans to choose against virtue and for vice. It results from the body's relationship to the material world and a desire to avoid pain and suffering. It pulls the conscience towards that which relieves the body of distress. It can and often does override the ability to choose virtue when acting on virtue would result in and/or increase pain and distress even when the same is a consequential necessity for achieving the character desired. The distress may be physical, mental, and/or emotional, or any combination of the three. A common athletic training mantra is the phrase *"No pain, no gain!"* It is a fundamental understanding of choosing pain when we perceive the value in advancing us toward our goal. It is also fundamental to developing our soul.

Making free-will choices followed by physical actions of the body is the essence of 'being' for humans. The life built-in body and spirit defines our character and move us on our journey from birth to natural death. Our Creator God did not leave us to this on our own. God's part is to guide us in forming our conscience and give us guideposts to help us know what we cannot discern for ourselves. God gave us the divine law to shape our comprehension of nature's law and enhance our understanding of natural law. This divine law comes to us through revelation through God's chosen people, Israel, the Law of Moses, and the prophets. Through the incarnation of God in Jesus of Nazareth, the messianic mission fulfills the Law and remakes God's covenant with us.

Remember, as we continue to walk this path the salvation mission of Jesus helps us renew our commitment to the Creator's gift of communion with Him and with each other. The mercy of Jesus's mission is that we can choose to repent and choose to renew our commitment to the covenant God made with us. Remember also His mercy, and remember while reading in prayer we are surrounded by angelic defenders.

**The Law – The Ten Commandments**
Civil society in this beginning of the twenty-first century has presented the Judeo-Christian Law of the Ten Commandments as restrictive, removing a person's freedom of choice and heavily regulating one's life away from pleasure and happiness. The value of these simple requirements written into our civil law is ignored by present day philosophies. The Truth of the Commandments' value to human living is this; they survived oral tradition for more than five hundred years before being written down in the sixth century B. C. and continued through another twenty-six hundred years to this day. The background these ten simple social rules is the survival of His chosen people in spite of the thousands of years of persecution and in the codifying of the values throughout Western society's civil law. The story of how the Commandments came to humans is chronicled in the Judeo-Christian scriptures of Genesis and Exodus. A summary follows here based on the scriptural reference.

The family of a man named Abraham lived in the hill country of what today is called Palestine/Israel. The family existed as Bedouins continue to survive even into this modern technical society, shepherding flocks and trading with those in their vicinities. Abraham was befriended by the Creator and passed his relationship and comprehension of God to his family. During the time of his grandson, Jacob, a famine took over the land. Food needed to be procured to assist in the survival of the family and flocks. Preceding the famine, the sons of Jacob became jealous of their brother Joseph because of their father's love for Joseph. They sold him off into slavery in Egypt, telling their father the boy was attacked and killed by a wild beast.

These sons of Jacob traveled to Egypt to seek the food and supplies they required for survival during a famine in their pasturelands. They were unaware that their brother Joseph was now the Vizier of Egypt, second in power only to the Pharaoh himself. Joseph maneuvered his brothers, who did not recognize him, into bringing their father and his holdings to Egypt, where Joseph had prepared the kingdom for the famine. Welcomed into

Egypt by one of such great political power, Jacob's family prospered and multiplied for generations.

Decades passed, and the succession of Pharaohs forgot the lessons and power of Joseph and recognized only that a great body of people called the Israelites were prosperous in their midst. Fearing an uprising, the later Egyptian Pharaohs enslaved Jacob's family and held them for several hundred years. Their freedoms were stripped. They were forbidden to worship in relationship with God. They were forced to labor to build temples and cities for the Pharaohs and the Egyptian gods. Among them rose a legend, a promise of one who would save them from slavery. One Pharaoh feared an uprising and had all the male children born in the past year killed.

One child was saved. He was called Moses because the woman who saved him, Pharaoh's daughter, drew him from the Nile River. He was raised as an Egyptian, discovered to be a Hebrew in his maturity, was exiled, and became the leader who would bring God's word to the new Pharaoh. This Pharaoh released the Israelites after enduring months of plagues and terrors visited on his people. Moses led the Israelites out of Egypt, after more than four-hundred years of slavery. However, enslaved people do not know how to govern themselves to form a community.

Though they had their own stories and legends, they were conditioned to know what the Egyptians told them regarding the rituals of the Egyptian gods. They recognized the tangible visible images of the Egyptian gods. This was the Israelites way of understanding their world. Though free of Egypt, they were not free. The Ten Commandments are a gift of freedom. They are a foundation for forming a community. They are a divine revelation, divine law, intended to free a people to worship God, give them guideposts to form their consciences, and live together in freedom.

Let's take fresh look at these Ten Commandments as social guidance in our own society. Let us consider them for the purpose of this journey, a journey on the formation of our own consciences with the intention of forming two-into-one in the sacramental union of marriage. What is it we are called *to do* and what is it we are called to *not do*. The following scriptures are from Exodus Chapter 20.

## *The Ten Commandments - The 'DOs'*

These first four Commandments form trust in a community. A pledge to divine law and to each other forms the foundation for a strong family, community, and nation.

*"I AM the Lord your God, who brought you out of the land of Egypt, out of slavery. You shall not have other gods beside me. You shall not make ... an idol or a likeness of anything...".*

You are free. Work with me, and nothing will enslave you; no one will bind you and keep you from me. Let nothing keep you from Me, not food, not libations, not chemical substances, or material goods command more attention from you than you give to me. You are free.

*"You shall not invoke the name of the Lord, your God, in vain".*

I AM the Creator God. You do not know my power. You cannot wield it. Respect this difference between us as we relate to each other, as a sign of love for each other.

*"Remember the sabbath day – keep it holy. Six days you may labor and do all your work, but the seventh day is a sabbath of the Lord your God".*

This is a day of rest and respite. It is a day of renewal. Join with others in renewing our community, our love relationship. I am giving you this gift. Please give it to yourselves as well.

*"Honor your father and mother".*

In The Beginning, you were commanded to be fruitful and multiply. Your parents fulfilled this command, and in love (however great or small), you were brought into the world to be with Me. Honor them, for they honored Me.

## *The 'DON'Ts'*

Action against the community breaks down the goodwill built in the first four commandments. This action changes the fundamental relationship of love and trust, and it must be avoided.

*"You shall not kill"*.
Killing another breaks down the community. Killing a life takes something that is not yours to take. All life belongs to Me. Killing a person does not stop with the body. Killing another's spirit, taking their life by killing their mind, their free choice, their conscience is the same as taking their body's life.

*"You shall not commit adultery"*.
In The Beginning, the woman was drawn from the man's side to be his partner. Not from his feet, that she would bow before him, and not from his head that she may lord over him. "and the two of them become one body"(Gn 2:24) each providing their given talent that they may become greater than their parts. Keep this dignity between you as a covenant sign of your relationship with Me. Once you choose, once you commit, do not mingle your intimacy with others.

*"You shall not steal"*.
I give you what you need. What I give to others is what they need. Be satisfied, and if not satisfied, use the talents I give you to learn, grow, and care. Consider that I may withhold something from you to give opportunity to another to care for you as part of the community.

### The 'DON'T even THINK about it'
The conscious consideration of ideas contrary to community opens the mind to concupiscence and is to be avoided. *This is a key point Jesus makes in Matthew's record of the Sermon on the Mount* .

*"You shall not bear false witness against your neighbor"*.
Telling the truth keeps the community strong. Telling a partial truth, bending the truth, or refusing to share the truth with the conscious intent to deceive is to break apart the community.

Lying kills the community. It is a prelude to breaking the fifth commandment.

*"You shall not covet your neighbor's wife"*.
Man and woman become one as a sign to the community of My love and relationship with the community. It is adultery to even think of breaking apart a holy bond (Mt 5:27).

*"You shall not covet your neighbor's goods"*.
Focusing on wanting another's talent or gifts is to spend time away from strengthening one's own. It is a cheat against the gifts awarded and the chance to increase those gifts to benefit oneself and the community. Coveting leads to breaking the seventh commandment.

The story of salvation history continues to unfold from these Ten Commandments through the First Covenant story. The Hebrew scriptures and the Christian Old Testament share the oral traditions, the gifts given to God's people woven into the stories, the verse, and the songs of the people. These gifts are relayed through the prophets, those teachers and leaders who counseled kings and taught the people, always with the intent of forming the inner heart to guide the outer actions. "Or if one loves righteousness, whose works are virtues, She teaches moderation and prudence, righteousness and fortitude, and nothing in life is more useful than these"(Wis 8:7).

### Virtue – the Seed and Fruit of Moral Acts
"Human virtues are firm attitudes, stable dispositions, habitual perfection of intellect and will that govern our actions, order our passions, and guide our conduct according to reason and faith. They create a semblance of ease, self-mastery, and joy in leading a morally good life. The virtuous one is one who freely practices the good"(CCC #1804).

Theological Virtues are *the framework* for building Cardinal (primary) Virtues. Theological Virtues are in the spirit of our being, waiting to be chosen by the work of our conscience in order that they may *guide our actions* through our journey. Faith is accepting the concept of human existence we have been describing. Our internal agreement is to step onto the path, living according to the truth of creation and the Creator's mission for us. Faith trusts the Word, the person and work of Jesus as the guidance for life here, leading toward life in eternity beyond here-and-now. Hope is the subsequent steps of the journey *along* this path. Hope is the ever-outreaching conscience seeking the continued support of the Divine's assistance in taking each step, often without knowing or understanding success is certain. Hope is a constant *"Yes!"* to the covenant relationship with God. Charity is the resulting action we take and our interaction with the Creator's world according to our understanding. Our free will choice results in a continuation of life and commitment that builds and supports the path for ourselves and as an example to others. "So faith, hope, love remain, these three; but the greatest of these is love"(1Cor13:13).

The *framework* for the path is the Theological Virtues. The vehicle we use to make our way down the path is the Cardinal or primary Virtues. All other virtues revert to these. One selecting to walk, jog, or run down the path would find these well-fitting shoes. A mechanic may call them tools, a sailor the favorite knot to bend on a sail, a quilter the favored needle and fabric, the way to create a warm embrace, a writer the pen-and-paper or shape of a keyboard. Choose a metaphor in place for your favorite as a reference.

Prudence is the tool of the right choice of conscience. Prudence is the gift that nudges us to move and in a direction supportive of our journey's end. It is at the same time motivation to do good, do well, and caution to avoid the sinful choice, keeping us on our mission and avoid misdirection from the path upon which we have set our feet. Prudence is the virtue calling us to look and compare what we know to be right and good and to choose to look at others for the same perspective of right and good. Prudence is a tool of rational thought. It is sacrificed when emotion clouds and even displaces the rational.

Justice is dual-edged as well. Justice is the affirmation of a 'right' choice made and the discipline, yes even the pain, to help us recognize when a poor choice is made. Justice is the rails on the side of the path. Justice is our understanding of the foundations of our conscience, of those beams and bricks we have used to direct our thoughts. We may choose to cross the rails of Justice at any time deviate from the path, considering the foundation may be flawed in formation. The thorns that prick, the rock that trips, the bog that slows, and the cliff that stops after we cross the rail will bring us an understanding of whether to rebuild or reaffirm the foundation. Justice must not be confused with revenge. All too often, the emotional response is what we perceive as injustice. 'That's not fair!' is the simple child's cry we feel in our emotions. To pursue revenge in the name of Justice is to run out into space past the edge of the cliff. Our tasks are to suffer the pain the emotion brings and remember the scripture "Vengeance is mine and recompense, for the time they lose their footing" (Dt 32:35). Stay on the path of the spiritual virtues.

Fortitude is the strength we draw from the spirit to continue along the path. It is also known as the grace from God. Fortitude draws on the habit of drinking from the sources of life upon which we formed our conscience. By this habit, we review the foundation of conscience. Fortitude is a cornerstone, a pillar of wisdom used to create the foundation. The Judeo-Christian resources are the first examples we are given from which to choose. The Christian family provides the experiences and practices leading us to Divine Law. We form the conscience through interaction with those walking along with us; parents, siblings, teachers, confessors, friends, priests, and wedding witnesses. Scripture reminds us of the right of these ancient-learned values. Fortitude is the practice of these and acting in accord with them strengthens our resolve to meet our covenant commitments.

Temperance pairs with Prudence. Temperance keeps us from strutting down the path at such a quick pace we forget the rails of Justice or the need to feed ourselves with the energy of Fortitude. Temperance reminds us to enjoy the journey, to use only what we need rather than everything we want. It tells us that the shoes are getting thin and need to be replaced with a new understanding. It tells us we need to feed and nurture our bodies, and to drink of virtue to nurture our spirits. Temperance keeps us from abusing the gifts given, to honor our spouses rather than to abuse them. Temperance urges us to engage in the goods of marriage for the unitive and procreative purposes those gifts provide, and to honor our spouse with prudent and just witness to our covenant.

These Theological and Cardinal Virtues are not the sole realm of Judeo-Christian thinking. The Apostles and Christian Fathers lived in a world formed by the Greeks and run by the Romans. They used this Greco-Roman philosophy of virtue to describe and expand the Gospel concepts into a society where civic and cultural foundations were laid by Alexander's empire and subsisted into Roman times. The Greeks taught of a human soul that was a shadow of something greater and outside the body and perished at death. In contrast, Hebrew Scriptures told of the Spirit of God, Wisdom, as a living sign within our persons and a promise of life of eternal happiness with the Creator. This life eternal sprouts first from Faith in the Divine, infused into the human spirit, continuing the circle of life in the garden world where we live.

## The Beatitudes – One Beginning of the Story of the New Covenant

Salvation History continues to its summit in the passion, death, and resurrection of Jesus. His public mission brought a summary testament of all the revelations to the Israelites. Jesus undertook to live a life exemplary of the Law and the Prophets and show us through His salvific act the end to which we all desire to progress, which is eternal life with the Creator God. Jesus spent three years in a public mission summarizing all that came before. Matthew, also called Levi, was a tax collector by profession. An educated man of his time, Matthew recorded the details of Jesus' mission in a manner most understandable to the Israelite/Jewish people. Matthew begins in earnest with Jesus on a mountain, reminding the Jews of Moses on Mount Sinai. Jesus gives the heart of the Law in the Beatitudes and explains a deeper meaning of the Ten Commandments. Our journey continues with the Beatitudes.

Father John Riccardo raises the modern social idea of The Beatitudes being a list for losers according to the twenty-first century civil society ("Why Be Good" Christ is the Answer program #753). Concepts of 'poor,' 'mourning,' being 'meek' as though helpless, giving 'mercy' as a sign of weakness, and so on are signs of humans' inability to manage themselves in a Darwinian world of survival of the fittest. No one would want to emulate these Christian values in their rational mind. Fr. Riccardo does this to call attention to the difference between contemporary philosophy of life in this third millennium and the Judeo-Christian tradition we are discussing.

The word 'blessed' may be translated from Greek to mean *fortunate* and *happy*. Happiness was defined at the beginning of our journey as a sense of contentment of character that ultimately results in eternal life in relationship with the Creator God. Therefore, those working toward or emulating these virtues live a *happy* life. The Beatitudes further define and lead us to happiness in our entire person; spirit, mind, and body. From Matthew chapter five, verses 3 – 12:

*"Blessed are the poor in spirit, for theirs is the kingdom of heaven."*
To emulate *poor in spirit* is to practice the virtue of Prudence and Temperance. It is knowing when one has *enough* for what one needs. To be poor in spirit is to avoid excesses of the *things of this world*, to learn to pass the wealth that one does not require and/or cannot redirect to the maintenance of the kingdom of God to others who need it or have the skills to distribute the wealth more effectively. Who would let the vegetables in the garden rot rather than pass them to a neighbor while they were fresh? (See the parable of the rich fool, Luke 12:16).

*"Blessed are they who mourn, for they will be comforted."*
Comforted by God, by the divine laws and Spirit of Love. Mourning may include despair, depression, confusion, and hurt. Learning and living these divine revelations provides a salve that raises one towards a life of happiness. Comfort is found in choosing to live by the Commandments and the Virtues' promise. Comfort brings contentment to those who return to the covenant path.

*"Blessed are the meek, for they will inherit the land."*
*Meek* is "enduring injury with patience and without resentment" (*Webster's Universal Encyclopedic Dictionary*. Federal Street Press, Barnes and Nobel Books. 2002. Print). Practicing meekness results in a disciplined conscience, a mind that holds the body's action toward an ordered life, an order bent toward the divine covenant to pursue happiness. It can be a difficult challenge, yet it is one necessary for those committed to marriage to develop and practice.

*"Blessed are they who hunger and thirst for righteousness, for they will be satisfied."*
Emphasize *righteousness* as with the virtue of Justice each has enough for what is needed. The Law is honored and followed by those in our company on the path. Those who do not choose a life in and for a relationship with God may violate this concept. Our responsibility is to remember that our examples may provide others with an inclination to join us. We must remain true to Justice and not replace Justice with revenge.

*"Blessed are the merciful, for they will be shown mercy."*
Jesus teaches us to pray "forgive us our debts as we forgive our debtors…" (Mt 5:9-13). Mercy is at the heart of daily living. Furthermore, emulating the Creator's image, we are commanded "You shall love your neighbor as yourself" (Mt 22:39). This pastoral message is echoed by Pope Francis. Mercy is teaching the value of the Law and the Virtues through an example first, and in the relationship of interaction with others both on and outside the path. Mercy is the action of conscience extending to the body's action, leaving open a gate to the path for those who repent.

*"Blessed are the clean of heart, for they shall see God."*
The Greeks thought the heart to be the center of the life of the body. Since the heart does drive the body's engine, here is where the energy of life was thought to reside. The mind and conscience have since been shown to be the source and center of life, the thinking and control function for the body. Here, in the conscience, creating habitual choice for good, the heart is cleansed. God can be found. Divine law is sensed.

*"Blessed are the peacemakers, for they will be called children of God."*
Those who are so gifted to discern the hearts of others and can bring others to peaceful action, preserving the wholeness of the community, have found the means to evangelize the world. All persons, the chosen people of Israel, Christians, and others who open themselves to the Divine are given this gift of sensing the hearts of others in some capacity. This grace leads us to offer our food to a stranger rather than throw a rock to chase them off, or turn to avoid meeting others along the paths we walk. We all have a great responsibility to bring together other people, whether within their households, between households, or between nation-states. This beatitude must be the perpetual open door between spouses at any point in their covenant marriage.

*"Blessed are they who are persecuted for the sake of righteousness, for theirs is the kingdom of heaven."*
Can one stand on the practice of virtues? Can one weather the storm of argument, bullying, mental challenge, and physical violence as received by the

world as a reward for practicing these virtues? Persecution tests the foundations of conscience against the storm of emotions trying to give rise to the cries of self-pity such as, "That's not fair" and of "Why me?" This Beatitude is a warning as much as it is a blessing, for there is more persecution to follow.

Matthew's account of Jesus' sermon shows Jesus bringing new perspective as preparation for following Him into His kingdom. There are traditionally eight Beatitudes taught in Christian catechisms. Perhaps it is too much to bear for many teachers to add this or too difficult for followers to believe when considering it. Did Jesus tell us to expect to suffer? This ninth beatitude tells us He did and still does today.

*"Blessed are you when they insult you and persecute you and utter every kind of evil against you [falsely] because of me. Rejoice and be glad, for your reward will be great in heaven."* [sic]

Look at how they treated the Savior, the Son of God. Those on the mountain that day in Galilee could not imagine what would become of the Lord. We look back and know it in all its horrors as recorded in the Gospel and as the historians have passed forward. Jesus was tortured for up to three days before being executed for defying the Sanhedrin and Rome's authorities. Even Rome's Senate eventually outlawed the use of crucifixion as punishment.

Nevertheless, martyrs sacrificed themselves for hundreds of years afterward rather than deny their faith in Jesus and The Way of life He taught. Jesus knew and the prophets before Him warned the Israelites of the trials they would face for living the Law, the Virtues, and the Beatitudes. Furthermore, He promised all, them and us, a reward of eternal life with Him when we live faithfully through our journey on this path.

The Christian perspective understands that the Beatitudes may be viewed in several ways. Fr. Riccardo's presentation demonstrates them as one portrait of Jesus. Each characteristic is evident in the Gospel through His words and works, providing us examples we may and should choose to live. For any Christian, the Commandments, descriptions of character through virtue, and the Beatitudes become the characteristics to build one's conscience. Choosing to take action according to these repeatedly further forms habits of one's conscience, making *right decisions* until they become reflected in habitual practice.

Christians live first with Jesus inside of themselves, and through the subsequent practice of action, brings Jesus to life for others.

### *Summation*
The purpose of taking time for this discussion is to create common ground for understanding the context of covenant marriage. We reminded ourselves of who and what we are, so we have a common reference as we move into the three-ply-cord subjects of covenant, speech, and healing. We are physical bodies with life breathed into us by God, giving us rational minds to make choices. Our free conscience discerns the choices to drive physical actions of the body. We observe nature's laws of being, as do the animals, and an additional innate desire to seek what is good. At the same time, the nature of the body includes concupiscent desire that drives us to select what is pleasurable and painless, beyond what we need and against what may be best for us. The Spirit of God breathed into us allows us to recognize God's divine law as we form our conscience. The habitual choice toward the good builds a stronger conscience. It drives actions that demonstrate the internal character of our minds and the intentions we select for our lives.

The Ten Commandments are a gift of life for communal living. Contrary to the perception of civil society, these laws were passed to us by our ancestors, who came through four centuries of slavery. They were told what to do and when for every action by their overlords. The Israelite community under Moses' leadership needed guidance for holding the very extended family together. Freedom was given to us through these circumstances, a freedom which comes from knowing the difference between a moral *right* and *wrong*. Through understanding these laws, we can build extended communities without fear.

The Virtues are both foundations for a spiritual life with God and foundational tools for interacting with God and others in this relationship of life. Faith, Hope, and Charity (Love) are graces we must choose first to believe. Our mental and physical actions of choice become guided by Prudence, Justice, Fortitude, and Temperance as resources feeding our purposes in bringing our work into reality. They provide the means for renewal, repentance, and resolution to continue our covenant commitment.

The Beatitudes are a portrait of Jesus Christ. They are a means for us to understand our progress in life and gage the quality of our consciences. These virtues move us toward strength in moral character to bring us happiness. At the end of our days, we anticipate an eternal life with the Creator God, through Jesus of Nazareth, the Christ, and in unity with the Holy Spirit of God as we live.

These concepts of Christian life are the foundation for the following sections of this work. The sections are set in an order consistent with building relationships and keeping them strong, allowing for healing when rifts are created. The commentary focuses on building and maintaining a Covenant Marriage according to Catholic pillars of Scripture and Tradition, understanding that these pillars begin in the roots of the Old Testament scriptures and tradition. Continuing your journey does not require, in fact, should not be worked as though this is a novel with a constructed beginning, middle, and end. It is for you, the reader, to decide where and how to work with the scripture and collected concepts. Remember, you do not walk alone.

Foremost, you walk through this with the Spirit of God. You are encouraged to work with and discuss the concepts and scriptures with others who hold Faith in the ideas previously shared. It is my hope you will be sharing with your fiancé or spouse in the company of a shared confessor to prepare or strengthen you on your journey together. Please do so with each other as your work inspires you.

If you come to this work in the confusion and torment of a broken covenant, I trust you have been inspired by the Creator. Let His Spirit continue to guide you through the work. Make certain you have a companion or two who also believe, as this chapter has described. It is intended to support your journey and be a companion in renewing and strengthening your covenant commitment.

Full and complete involvement in the work is encouraged by writing down personal thoughts, both rational and emotional. This is psychology of learning, a reinforcement of your thoughts and a creative memory aid, for reference should you return looking for an idea or affirming an idea in your mind. Writing completes the action of the conscience, creating in reality that which the mind works on, deciphers, and yearns to make real. It may be therapeutic as well.

Grace and peace be in your hearts as you move further along your path through this work.

## Concepts of Covenant

Do you remember your best friend from when you were an eight-year-old? How about the best friend when you were twelve? Seventeen? When you made your marriage vows? How about today, while you read this. Who is your best friend? How long have you been best friends? Now, who is your oldest friend? When was the last time you spoke with them?

The next question is "What made you best friends?". Likely, it was some combination of interweaving interests, social group involvement, or a critical event in your life when you shared common experiences and emotions. Pause here, and take some time to look into your reasons.

You will likely find that what you believed in was tested, and the two of you came through the experience with a common outlook or position. "These are the times that try men's' souls," was the opening line written by an American patriot Thomas Paine. It was December 1776, and the American Revolution was only beginning. A cold, hard winter lay ahead for most of the Colonies. "My God, my God, why have you abandoned me?" (Ps 22:2) was the cry of Jesus from the cross just before He expired. His mother and His best friend, John, suffered through this together. Trials great and small test the virtue of Faith in our consciences.

Life-long friendship tests the faith and principles to which we bind ourselves. Life is transient. Our neighbors change, one or the other moving away—our social group changes due to interests and new pursuits being sought. We change jobs and careers, and those we once lived with day-to-day are no longer the same. We have memories of common experiences that tested us, and we engage in new experiences with other people. We affirm or change our views and principles with these others and lose the opportunities to share with new with former friends.

A covenant is an agreement between friends to continue to share common experiences and considerations of the same. A covenant is a solemn agreement between us, as embodied spirits, between friends to keep our communication and experiences in common by sharing them. The covenant between God and humankind is the model for this commitment. It was created in the Garden. Like all things, it was created to be *very good*. The Genesis story is the model for our covenant commitment to our best friends, especially to our spouse, that we will witness and share our lives. Our Godly covenant is renewed continuously in scripture; Noah (Gn Ch. 9), Moses and the Israelites (Ex Ch.20), Samuel (Sm Ch. 3), David (2Sm 5:1 – 5), and the Jews (Neh 8:1 – 12) are some of the many examples. Jesus fulfills and provides for continual renewal of the covenant through the acts of His passion, death, and resurrection. It is renewed by each of us when we say 'yes' to Him through the act of receiving the Eucharist. "By the Eucharistic celebration we already unite ourselves with the heavenly liturgy and anticipate eternal life, when God will be all in all" (CCC 1Cor 15:28). This covenant is the commitment intended in marriage.

Covenant is defined throughout the scriptures. The Bible is the covenant bond between God and His people, the Groom and His Bride. Covenant marriage is evident in scripture from the beginning. Adam was directed to cling to Eve. Abraham was faithful to Sari into her advanced age. His grandson Jacob gave fourteen years of servitude to demonstrate his faithful intent to Rachel. Song of Songs is a love sonnet between a groom and his betrothed and Proverbs 31 is the author's blessing of the character of his wife. Jesus told the Pharisees to recall Genesis when pressed about divorce. Paul wrote chapters about the development of Christian marriage expectations to include family and social interactions in his letters to the Corinthians and Ephesians. Revelation closes with a wedding.

The social construct of marriage in Western society has deviated from this definition. In less than a century, divorce-on-demand has become legally and socially acceptable to the majority in spite the Gospel message. Marriage has been legislated away from the Judeo-Christian concept practiced over three thousand years of development and understanding of marriage as a covenant. Legal, social, and theological critics point out that the Catholic Church did not codify marriage law until the eleventh century, questioning the Church's authority and marriage-as-sacrament as a point of argument. Forgotten is how Roman law concerning marriage and family faded from memory as the empire came apart. Where Rome's civil authority waned, moral guidance was necessary to preserve the sanctity of the family and The Church continued to present this guidance in both civil and religious practice under Judeo-Christian principles.

At this beginning of the twenty-first century, there is no doubt that marriage as covenant (rather than contract) is counter-cultural. We are handicapped in our vision of marriage in this age. There persists an ancient pagan sense that the woman is a man's property. Western culture enforces this, particularly the Victorian English social construct in North America. Fighting this idea, a feminist movement tells women they are not women unless they can do what men do. Anything less falls into the former categories. And, new social constructs distort with great success the differences between man and woman to a point where some live as the other while others take extreme action and surgically attempt to change their bodies. The guidance of scripture is lost to the collective conscience.

This chapter is dedicated to renewing knowledge of just how different the Judeo-Christian religious view marriage is from Western social concepts and civil law. Through scripture, an understanding of covenant is reviewed. Judaism is the root of Christianity. The First Covenant of the Old Testament presents God's intent for covenant relationship. Christians followed Jesus' teaching and later the authors of the Gospel acts as they recorded His teachings. The Apostles' records in the New Testament writings reveal their efforts to follow Jesus' renewal. Today, the guidance of covenant marriage is the principle upon which we base the building of family and home.

We are made of the same substance, we men and women, "…bone of my bones and flesh of my flesh" (Gn 2:23). Preceding this, humans are shown to be made of 'clay,' the stuff of the earth, and given life not only by God's divine command but also by the mighty divine breath. Such is the root of the dignity of the human being. The man "leaves his father and mother and clings to his wife..." (Gn 2:24). To cling is "to hold or hold on tightly or tenaciously" (www.merriam-webster.com/dictionary/cling. Dictionary.com, LLC. 2022. On-line.). He, the man, is supposed to cling to her, to hold her in esteem.

The intimacy of the mingling of the human body cannot be an obscurity in the age of science. The romance of holding hands, walking arm-in-arm, kissing, the intimacy of sexual intercourse, and creating new life is held dearly in our minds and nature. Veiled in the idea of a simple toothbrush left at a lover's home, the plain biological activities of life are evident in society; the shared use of tub and shower, and the cup at the sink, tableware and towels, and others are shared items of life that bind us as one person. We don't discuss those small intimacies of life and even less the principles of living that are points of decision-making. Marriage means we work at making our bodies *and* minds one through the same sources of inspiration with which we make wise decisions. These efforts in thought and action define the divine and spiritual meaning of 'Love.' Man and woman are intended to be joined in body, mind, and spirit through virtues and beatitudes.

It is not necessary to take a marriage vow in a church building. Every society on earth has some form of marital union. Common-Law marriage was upheld in the United States law (see Dubler, A. The Yale Law Journal, Vol. 107, No. 6 April, 1998) as an agreement between a man and a woman (see Lind. G. *"Common Law Marriage: A Legal Institution for Cohabitation"*. Abstract accessed Oxford Scholarship Online, March 2022). Modern laws across the globe recognize marriage as a financial contract. In certain societies, marriage contracts are still made to strengthen familial ties and tribal bonds for various purposes. Distorted definitions of *love*, often driven by emotional and instinctual attractions, drive the concept leading to the practice of marriage between consenting parties. Variations change with the desires of humanity to act by personal whims and desires removed from natural and moral norms and laws.

A marriage vow before God intends a marriage based on the principles discussed in chapter one. Under the yoke of Christian discipline, those who commit themselves to marriage commit to a covenant rather than a contract. The meaning of covenant is a chosen protective act towards the other *under any circumstance*. A covenant requires a party to think and act in a manner that best suits the other party.[1] Before God, the parties to a marriage promise to do everything possible to bring the other to our ultimate end; life in God for eternity. This is the goal of the Christian life. This is what a man and woman committing to the marriage covenant promise each other.

The decision to enter such a covenant must first be a free decision of the individual man and the woman. There can be no impediment, no restrictions, and no forceful pending actions. Each must make the decision and have some vision for an eternal commitment. There can be no hesitations in mind and no formal contractual releases. These would entail contracts rather than covenant commitment. There can be no penalty for choosing not to marry. No pregnancy, joining of kingdoms nor *shot-gun* enticements can interfere with a free decision.

Faithfulness to the commitment is necessary to maintain the integrity of the covenant. Faithfulness in the binding of the two wills. It is the shield against all that would work to pull the covenant apart. Faithfulness allows for strengthening when events and influences of the world beat on the two to pull them apart.

Trust is at the core of this faithfulness, knowing in one's heart and remembering that the end goal of the covenant is eternal life for the other.

Producing 'fruit' is the natural outgrowth and expansion of true love. The first fruit comes from serving the other. A husband and wife support each other's work and join their skills and efforts. The result is the new entity greater than a simple sum of the two. A common home and service to the community work jointly to support immediate and extended families. The fruit of children must also be intended, where the joining of minds and bodies produce, nurture, and raise new generations to understand and work in and with the concept of covenant.

A covenant, by definition, is forever. The commitment made by the man and the woman must be intended to last until God calls one or both home to

---

[1] Circumstances arise from antiquity through today where human frailty breaks the normal healthy conduct of conscience. Consideration and action for civil divorce can be the best course of action in some situations. The focus here remains on the concept that spouses continue to honor the covenant in the treatment of the other. This is a difficult, counter-cultural ask in a civil world of divorce on demand where spouses *remain friends*, then break the vows of fidelity and forever by marrying another. "For better or for worse" is overridden.

heaven from this Garden. The world surrounding the two will continually test this part of the vow. The world outside of covenant commitment makes provisions for specifically breaking this part of the vows. Should one falter from their covenant commitment, the other must persist. For in God's time, it may be that the faithful one will still preserve the life's love commitment that will bring the fallen one to heaven. More and more, this faithfulness is needed as an example of the service sacramental love.

How often is a proposal made with this fervor of intention? The opening story of this chapter offered one romantic ideal. Through these pages, we explored a depth of concept not often part of the euphoria of courtship. Chapter 5 describes the four specific wedding vows of the sacrament in more detail. The following pages provide consolidated access to scriptures for spiritual strength for those who desire to commit to a sacramental, covenant marriage. It is also intended as a means for enhancing those already committed. I pray that all who venture to read will find the grace of God flowing into their hearts.

# The First Covenant Scriptures

*Genesis 2:21 – 25 "So the Lord God cast a deep sleep on the man, and while he was asleep, he took at one of his ribs and closed up its place with flesh. The Lord God then builds up into a woman the rib which he had taken from the man. When he brought her to the man, the man said, "This one, at last, is bone of my bones and flesh of my flesh; This one shall be called 'woman' for out of 'her man' this one has been taken. That is why a man leaves his father and mother and clings to his wife, and the two of them become one body. The man and wife were both naked and they felt no shame."*

*Gn 9: 1, 7, 8, , 11, 13 Covenant with Noah*

"*God blessed Noah and his sons and said to them: Be fertile and multiply and fill the earth.*"

"*Be fertile, then, and multiply; abound on earth and subdue it.*"

"*God said to Noah and to his sons with him: See, I am now establishing my covenant with you and your descendants after you and with every living creature that was with you:…*"

"*I will establish my covenant with you, that never again shall all creatures be destroyed by the waters of a flood;…*"

"*I set my bow in the clouds, to serve as a sign of the covenant between me and the earth.*"

*Gn 12: 1 – 4 "The Lord Said to Abram: Go forth from your land, your relatives, and from your father's house to a land that I will show you. I will make of you a great nation, and I will bless you; I will make your name great, so that you will be a blessing. I will bless those who bless you and curse those who curse you. All the families of the earth will find blessing in you. Abram went as the Lord directed him,…"*

*Gn 12: 7 – The Lord said: To your descendants I will give this land. So Abram built an altar there to the Lord who had appeared to him."*

*Gn 15:1, 2, 5, 6*

*"Some time afterward, the word of the Lord came to Abram in a vision: "Do not fear, Abram! I am your shield; I will make your reward very great." But Abram said, "Lord God, what can you give me, if I die childless and have only a servant of my household,"* …*He took him outside and said: "Look up at the sky and count the stars, if you can. Just so, he added, will your descendants be. Abram put his faith in the Lord, who attributed it to him as an act of righteousness."*

*Gn 17: 1-7, 9*

*"…the Lord appeared to Abram and said: "I am God the Almighty. Walk in my presence and be blameless. Between you and me I will establish my covenant, and I will multiply you exceedingly." Abram fell face down and God said to him: For my part, here is my covenant with you: you are to become the father of a multitude of nations. No longer will you be called Abram; your name will be Abraham, for I am making you the father of a multitude of nations. I will maintain my covenant between me and you and your descendants after you throughout the ages as an everlasting covenant, to be your God and the God of your descendants after you. "For your part, you and your descendants after you must keep my covenant throughout the ages.*

*Gn 18: 20, 23*

"So the Lord said: The outcry against Sodom and Gomorrah is so great, and their sin so grave, that I must go down to see whether or not their actions are as bad as the cry against them that comes to me. I mean to find out." Then Abraham drew near and said: "Will you really sweep away the righteous with the wicked? Suppose there are fifty righteous people in the city;…"

*Ex 20: 1 – 17*
*The God Spoke all these words:*
*"I am the Lord your God, who brought you out of the land of Egypt, out of the house of slavery. You shall not have other gods beside me. You shall not make for yourself an idol or likeness of anything in the heavens above or on the earth below or in the waters beneath the earth; you shall not bow down before them or serve them. For I, the Lord, your God, am a jealous God, inflicting punishment for their ancestors' wickedness on the children of those who hate me, down to the third and fourth generations, but showing love down to the thousandth generation of those who love me and keep my commandments."*

*"You shall not invoke the name of the Lord, your God, in vain." For the Lord will not leave unpunished anyone who invokes his name in vain."*

*"Remember the sabbath day – keep it holy. Six days you may labor and do all your work, but the seventh day is a sabbath of the Lord your God. You shall not do any work, either you, your son, or your daughter,…For in six days the Lord made the heavens and the earth, the sea and all that is in them; but on the seventh day he rested. That is why the Lord has blessed the sabbath day and made it holy."*

*"Honor your father and your mother, that you may have long life in the land the Lord your God is giving you."*

*"You shall not kill."*

*"You shall not commit adultery."*

*"You shall not steal."*

*"You shall not bear false witness against your neighbor."*

*"You shall not covet your neighbor's house. You shall not covet your neighbor's wife,… or anything that belongs to your neighbor."*

A Three-Ply Cord

(intentionally blank for reader's notations)

*Deuteronomy 23:22* "*When you make a vow to the Lord, your God, you shall not delay in fulfilling it; otherwise you will be held guilty, for the Lord, your God, is strict in requiring it of you.*"

*Ruth 1:16 – 18* "*But Ruth said, "Do not press me to go back and abandon you! wherever you go I will go, wherever you lodge I will lodge. Your people shall be my people and your God, my God. Where you die I will die, and there be buried. May the Lord do thus to me, and more, if even death separates me from you?" Naomi then ceased to urge her, for she saw she was determined to go with her.*"

The Book 'The Wisdom of Sirach' or 'Ben Sira' is a father's advice to his son. It is easily perceived as patristic in an era when feminism is prominent. However, scripture is for all and the advice and caution given a son is important for daughters as well.

*Sirach 6:5 – 7, 14 – 17:* "*Pleasant speech multiplies friend, and gracious lips, friendly greetings. Let those who are friendly to you be many, but one in a thousand your confidant. When you gain friends, gain them through testing, and do not be quick to trust them.*

*Faithful friends are a sturdy shelter, whoever finds one finds a treasure. Faithful friends are beyond price, no amount can balance their worth. Faithful friends are a life-saving medicine; those who fear God will find them. Those who fear the Lord enjoy stable friendship, for as they are, so will their neighbors be.*"

*Sirach 7:19, 26 "Do not reject a sensible wife, a gracious wife is more precious than pearls." "…do not mistreat her, but do not trust the wife you hate."*

*Proverbs 10:12 "Hatred stirs up disputes, but lover covers all offenses."*
*Proverbs 11:16 "A gracious woman gains esteem…"*
*Proverbs 12:4 "A woman of worth is the crown of her husband,…"*

# A Three-Ply Cord

*Proverbs 31:10 – 31 Poem on the Woman of Worth*
*"Who can find a woman of worth? Far beyond jewels is her value.*
*Her husband trusts her judgment, he does not lack income.*
*She brings him profit, not loss, all the days of her life.*
*She seeks out wool and flax and weaves with skillful hands.*
*Like a merchant fleet she secures her provisions from afar.*
*She rises while it is still night, and distributes food to her household, a portion to her maidservants.*
*She picks out a field and acquires it, from her earnings she plants a vineyard.*
*She girds herself with strength; she exerts her arms with vigor.*
*She enjoys the profit from her dealings, her lamp is never extinguished at night.*
*She puts her hands to the distaff, and her fingers ply the spindle.*
*She reaches out her hands to the poor, and extends her arms to the needy.*
*She is not concerned for her household when it snows – all her charges are doubly clothed.*
*She makes her own coverlets, fine linen and purple are her clothing.*
*Her husband is prominent at the city gates as he sits with the elders of the land.*
*She makes garments and sells them, and stocks the merchants with belts.*
*She is clothes with strength and dignity and laughs at the days to come.*
*She opens her mouth in wisdom, kindly instruction is on her tongue.*
*She watches over the affairs of her household, and does not earth the bread of idleness.*
*Her children rise up and call her blessed; her husband, too, praises her.*
*Many are the women of proven worth, but you have excelled them all.*
*Charm is deceptive and beauty fleeting; the woman who fears the Lord is to be praised.*
*Acclaim her for the work of her hands, and let her deeds praise her at the city gates."*

JOHN LOUIS

(intentionally blank for reader's notations)

*Song of Solomon, Song of Songs, Canticle of Canticles*
Eight chapters of poetry intensely describing the aching of a woman's heart for her lover is the love sonnet of all love sonnets. It measures the depths of spiritual longing and teases the erotic yearnings of the body, and rightly so as the conjugal union and children are the desired ends of marriage. Would that all who wonder about love breathe this poem into their hearts and let it remain the eternal fire to be kindled and relit throughout life together! Open your personal study bible and prayerfully engage this work!

*Tobit 8: 4 – 8 "Tobiah rose from bed and said to his wife, "My sister, come, let us pray and beg our Lord to grant us mercy and protection." She got up and they started to pray and beg that they might be protected. He began with these words:*

> *"Blessed are you, O God of our ancestors; Blessed be your name forever and ever! Let the heavens and all your creation bless you forever. You made Adam, and you made his wife Ever to be his helper and support; and from these two the human race has come."*
>
> *"You said , 'It is not good for man to be alone; let us make a helper like himself.' Now, not with lust. but with fidelity I take this kinswoman as my wife. Send down your mercy and me and on her, and grant that we may grow old together. Bless us with children."*
>
> *And together, they said "Amen!"*

*Sirach 6:6-7; 14 – 17 Let those who are friendly to you be many, but one in a thousand your confidant." "Faithful friends are a sturdy shelter; whoever finds one finds a treasure. Faithful friends are beyond price, no amount can balance their worth. Faithful friends are life-saving medicine; those who fear God will find them. Those who fear the Lord enjoy stable friendship, for as they are, so will their neighbors be."*

The whole of chapter six of the Wisdom of Ben Sira (Sirach) is worthy of our time to understand how to find and build around us a group of trusted friends.

*Sirach 7:19* – "*Do not reject a sensible wife, a gracious wife is more precious than pearls.*"

# A Three-Ply Cord

*Sirach 9:1 - 9*
*"Do not be jealous of the wife of your bosom, lest you teach her to do evil against you.*
*Do not give a woman power over you to trample your dignity.*
*Do not go near a strange woman lest you fall into her snares.*
*Do not dally with a singer lest you be captivated by her charms.*
*Do not entertain thoughts about a virgin, lest you be enmeshed in damages for her.*
*Do not give yourself to a prostitute lest you lose your inheritance.*
*Do not look around the streets of the city, nor wander through its squares.*
*Avert your eyes from a shapely woman; do not gaze upon a beauty that is not yours.*
*Through woman's beauty many have been ruined, for love of it burns like fire.*
*Never recline at table with a married woman, or drink intoxicants with her, Lest your heart be drawn to her and you go down in blood to the grave."*

*Sirach 9:10 – Do not abandon old friends; new ones cannot equal them. A new friend is like new wine - when it has aged, you drink it with pleasure."*

*Sirach 18:22, 23 – Let nothing prevent the prompt payment of your vows: do not wait until death to fulfill them. Before making a vow prepare yourself; do not be like one who puts the Lord to the test."*

*Sirach 22:21, 22 – "Should you draw a sward against a friend, do not despair, for it can be undone. Should you open your mouth against a friend, do not worry, for you can be reconciled."*

*Sirach 26:1 – 4 –* "*Happy the husband of a good wife; the number of his days will be doubled. A loyal wife brings joy to her husband and he will finish his years in peace. A good wife is a generous gift bestowed upon men who fear the Lord. Whether rich or poor, his heart is content, a smile ever on his face.*"

*Sirach 26:13 – 18 – "A gracious wife delights her husband, her thoughtfulness puts flesh on his bones. A silent wife is a gift from the Lord, nothing is worth more than her self-discipline. A modest wife is a supreme blessing, no scales can weigh the worth of her chastity. The sun rising in the Lord's heaven – the beauty of a good wife in her well-ordered home. The light which shines above the holy lampstand – a beautiful face on a stately figure. Golden columns on silver bases – so her shapely legs and steady feet."*

# A Three-Ply Cord

*Sirach 27:17, 21 – Cherish your friend, keep faith with him;..." "For a wound can be bandaged, and an insult forgiven,..."*

*Sirach 36:26 – 29 – "A woman's beauty makes her husband's face light up, for it surpasses all else that delights the eye. An if, besides, her speech is soothing, her husband's lot is beyond that of mortal men. A wife is her husband's richest treasure, a help like himself and a staunch support."*

(End Old (First) Testament Section

# New Covenant Scriptures

*Mt 19:4 – 6 – He said in reply, "Have you not read that from the beginning the Creator 'made them male and female' and said, 'For this reason a man shall leave his father and mother and be joined to his wife, and the two shall become one flesh'? So they are no longer two, but one flesh. Therefore, what God has joined together, no human being must separate."*

*Mk 10:6 – 9 – But from the beginning of creation, 'God made them male and female. For this reason a man shall leave his father and mother and be joined to his wife, and the two shall become one flesh. So they are no long two but one flesh. Therefore what God has joined together, no human being must separate."*

*1Cor7:2 – 5 – It is a good thing for a man not to touch a woman, but because of cases of immorality every man should have his own wife, and every woman her own husband. The husband should fulfill his duty toward his wife and likewise the wife toward her husband. A wife does not have authority over her own body, but rather her husband, and similarly a husband does not have authority over his own body, but rather his wife. Do not deprive each other, except perhaps by mutual consent for a time, to be free for prayer, but then return to one another, so that Satan may not temp you through your lack of self control."*

*1Cor7:10, 11* – *"To the married, however, I give this instruction (not I, but the Lord): A wife should not separate from her husband – and if she does separate she must either remain single or become reconciled to her husband – and a husband should not divorce his wife."*

*1 Cor 13:4 – 8 –* "*Love is patient, love is kind. It is not jealous, {love} is not pompous, it is not inflated, it is not rude, it does not seek its' own interests, it is not quick-tempered, it does not brood over injury, it does not rejoice over wrong doing but rejoices with the truth. It bears all things, believes all things, hopes all things, endures all things. Love never fails.*"

*Eph 5:21 – 31* – *"Be subordinate to one another out of reverence for Christ. Wives should be subordinate to their husbands as to the Lord. For the husband is head of his wife just as Christ is head of the church, he himself the savior to the body. As the church is subordinate to Christ, so wives should be subordinate to their husbands in everything. Husbands, love your wives, even as Christ loved the church and handed himself over for her to sanctify her, cleansing her by the bath of water with the word, that he might present himself the church in splendor, without spot or wrinkle or any such thing, that she might be holy and without blemish. So [also] husbands should love their wives as their own bodies. He who loves his wife loves himself,. For no one hates his own flesh but rather nourishes and cherishes it, even as Christ does the church, because we are members of his body. "For this reason a man shall leave [his] father and [his] mother and be joined to his wife, and the two shall become one flesh."*

*Col 3:18 – 21 – The Christian Family "Wives, be submissive to your husbands, as is proper in the Lord. Husbands, love your wives, and avoid any bitterness toward them. Children, obey your parents in everything, for this is pleasing to the Lord. Fathers, do not provoke your children, so they may not become discouraged."*

# Speaking – The Divine Gift of Creation

The embodied spirit created by God encompasses the ability to use critical thinking (reason) to determine what actions we take. This action of the Will drives physical habits. Choosing which of the ideas coming into our minds allows us to guide the actions of our physical nature. This divine gift is beyond animal instinct. It is what sets Man apart from other animals. Reasoning, the act of critical thinking, is the work of the conscience, the intersection of the spirit and the body. It extends the ancient concept of what it means to be a *human* being. Before we speak, and by speaking commit to covenant life, it is critical to understand the reality of what it means to be made in the image of God. These ideas are ancient, long understood by humanity. This concept is key to beginning contemplation and understanding the scriptures to follow.

"In the beginning…" God *said, called, blessed,* and *commanded* sixteen times. The story is narrated. There is no poetry or prose. The writers present God speaking. To speak is an act of divine creation. We are given a gift to participate in that very act of creation. Two of the Ten Commandments regard the use of speech. "Thou shalt not invoke the name of the Lord thy God in vain" and "Thou shalt not bear false witness against thy neighbor" (Ex 20: 7, 16) are intended to discipline our use of this divine gift, that what we say will create only something that God can hear and see as *good*.

Jesus reminded us of the nature of the connection between thinking and speaking when teaching about adultery at the Sermon on the Mount. "You have heard that it was said, 'You shall not commit adultery.' But I say to you, everyone who looks at a woman with lust has already committed adultery with her in his heart" (Mt 5:27, 28). The complete Sermon is more than the Beatitudes. It is a full lesson on how actions begin in what the ancients called our *heart*. This lesson was so important that Matthew gave three full chapters of his record to share Jesus' details about following the Commandments, warning about taking oaths, loving rather than retaliating against enemies, about how to pray (a mental activity), about how to fast (a physical activity), and more than a dozen other lessons about living the Beatitudes. The life of a Christian begins in the conscience, in the *heart*.

St. Augustine followed in the fourth century when he wrote, "You made the workman's body for him; his mind able to command his limbs…[that] he may convey what he does from mind to the material, and report it back, so that his mind may consult the truth… within it, whether it is done well or not" (Confessions XI:5). Augustine's work in *Confessions* is a complete example of his understanding of these words. The writing of his autobiography is the cycle of thinking of his life, his sins, his faults, writing them down, examining them, and leaving for God whether what Augustine's heart has become is done well or not. The work traveled through the centuries to us as an example of this image of how we may reflect on how well we emulate the divine image.

St. Thomas Aquinas followed Augustine's line of thought during the twelfth century in his work, writing "…what is principle in man is said to be man; sometimes, indeed, the intellectual part which, in accordance with truth, is called the 'inward' man; and sometimes the sensitive part with the body is called man in the opinion of those whose observation does not go beyond the senses. And this is called the 'outward' man" [sic] (Aquinas, T. "*Summa Theologia Prima Part Q 75 Art. 4 Reply Obj. 1*" Knight, K. Ed. NewAdvent.org. 2017. On-line). Human beings have some quality of an intellectual part within themselves. Every human being acts through the sensitive outward part called the body that perceives and responds to the world. St. Thomas is reminding his peers and students of the fundamental make-up of human beings, spiritual (intellectual) and physical (sensual).

St. Pope John Paul the Great held to this principle when he directed the writing of the encyclical letter Veritatis Splendor in August of 1993. The *Splendor of Truth* is an instructive letter to the Church that reminds us of our ability to know the difference between good and evil. Jesus' redemptive act completed the healing of humanity after Adam and Eve's disobedience for eating from the Tree. "Truth enlightens man's intelligence and shape his freedom, leading him to know and love the Lord" (VS Blessing). Reason, *that critical thinking of the intellect*, is the beginning of the work of discipleship in our minds before we act. *Loving* results from *right thinking* turned into *right action*, and *speaking* reveals to others the intention and purpose driving our actions.

Augustine, Aquinas, and John Paul II are only three of the many theological waypoints through two-thousand years of Christian thought. They affirm the concept of the embodied spirit that is the reality of being human. Teaching and practicing carry the ideals through time. These ideals become the fundamental examples, the Tradition that is the Gospel the Church teaches, necessary to continue to form them as social norms of daily life.

Consider adding a bit of yeast to flour, water, and egg and the difference it makes between a flatbread and leavened loaf. Flatbread is food for an uncertain journey as when the Exodus from Egypt occurred. The Ten Commandments are the bread and water of conscience that sustained a community in the desert of social formation. Speaking in marriage forms and reaffirms the for the community the vows of covenant commitment. The Virtues shared in common add flavor and adhesion to the mix, holding together an improved social construct. Yeast is the ingredient for the bread of feast and celebration. The Beatitudes are yeast, causing the relationship to rise about the sum of all the parts. This is the bread we share in our marriages. It is full of the Truth of the life to nourish our journey together. Scripture becomes the leaven that lifts and builds Reason in our minds. *We build* the structure of Truth into our conscience, following the lofty ideals our teachers share with us, and through the continuous routine of reading and responding to scripture.

Finally, prayer spoken together is the warmth that gives energy to the yeast of Truth. Prayer and scripture are as husband and wife, two parts of the same divine image. Joint prayer is the receptacle for the Holy Spirit, where God's guidance is received. Jesus tells us, "…do not worry about what you are to say. But say whatever will be given to you at that hour. For it will not be you who are speaking but the holy Spirit" (Mk 13:11). From good-night through the next day to the following good-night, we speak of and to our spouses. We speak of our love, we speak of the weather, and we speak of the family business. Let our words, from vows spoken in front of witnesses through each word we present, be created with heart-filled intent that they can remain secure and become the outward sign of the sacramental covenant.

It matters what principles our conscious Will selects in directing our words. The following Abrahamic and Gospel religious principles are divine gifts to consider and employ while building our humanity. This chapter is intended to help you understand the principles of the Old Testament and New Testament scriptures where the use of speech is important to our discipleship and as directed specifically toward creating a covenant marriage.

# The First Covenant Scriptures

*Genesis 1:3 - 5 "Then God said: Let there be light, and there was light. God saw that the light was good. God called the light "day, " and the darkness he called "night."*
*Gn 1:6, 8 "The God said: Let there be a dome in the middle of the waters, to separate one body of water from the other. God called the dome sky."*
*Gn 1:9, 10 "Then God said: Le the water under the sky be gathered into a single basin, so that the dry land may appear. Cod called the dry land "earth, " and the basin of water he called "sea."*
*Gn 1:11 "Then God said: Let the earth bring forth vegetation…"*
*Gn 1:14 "Then God said: Let there be lights in the dome of the sky, to separate day from night."*
*Gn 1:20, 22 "Then God said: Let the water teem with an abundance of living creatures, and on the earth let birds fly…and God blessed them saying: Be fertile, multiply,…"*
*Gn 1:24 "Then God said: Let the earth bring forth every kind of living creature:…*
*Gn 1:26, 28 "Then God said: Let us make human beings in our image, after our likeness. God blessed them and God said to them: Be fertile and multiply; fill the earth and subdue it."*

*Genesis 2:19* "*So the Lord God formed out of the ground all the wild animals and all the birds of the air, and he brought them to the man to see what he would call them; whatever the man called each living creature was then its name.*"

*Ex 20:7 –* "*You shall not invoke the name of the Lord, your God, in vain. For the Lord will not leave unpunished anyone who invokes his name in vain.*"

*Ex 20:16 –* "*Thou shalt not bear false witness against your neighbor.*"

*Jos 6:20* "*As the horns blew, the people began to shout. When they heard the sound of the horn, they raised a tremendous shout,. The wall collapsed,…*"

*Ps 12:3 – 5 – "They tell lies to one another, speak with deceiving lips and a double heart. May the Lord cut off all deceiving lips, and every boastful tongue, Those who say, "By our tongues we prevail: when our lips speak, who can lord it over us?"*

*Psalm 15:1 – 5* – *"Lord, who may abide in your tent? Who may dwell on your holy mountain? Who walks without blame, doing what is right, speaking truth from the heart; Who does not slander with the tongue, does no harm to a friend, never defames a neighbor,…Who keeps an oath despite the cost,…Whoever acts like this shall never be shaken."*

*Ps 34:14* "…*Keep your tongue from evil, your lips from speaking lies."*
(see 1 Pt 3:10)

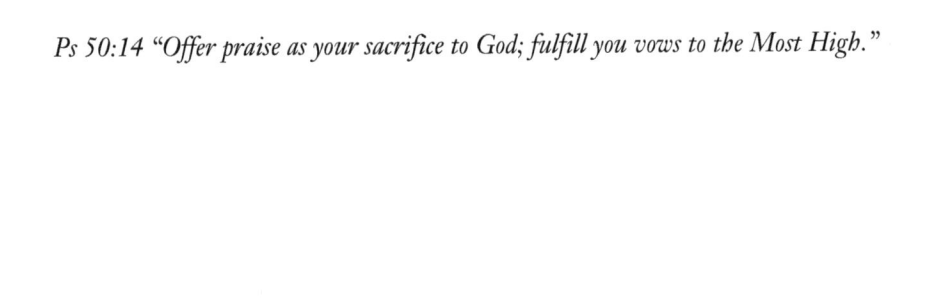

*Ps 50:14 "Offer praise as your sacrifice to God; fulfill you vows to the Most High."*

*Ps 52:3 – 6 – "All day long you are thinking up intrigues; your tongue is like a sharpened razor, you worker of deceit. You love evil more than good, lying rather than saying what is right. You love all the words that create confusion, you deceitful tongue.*

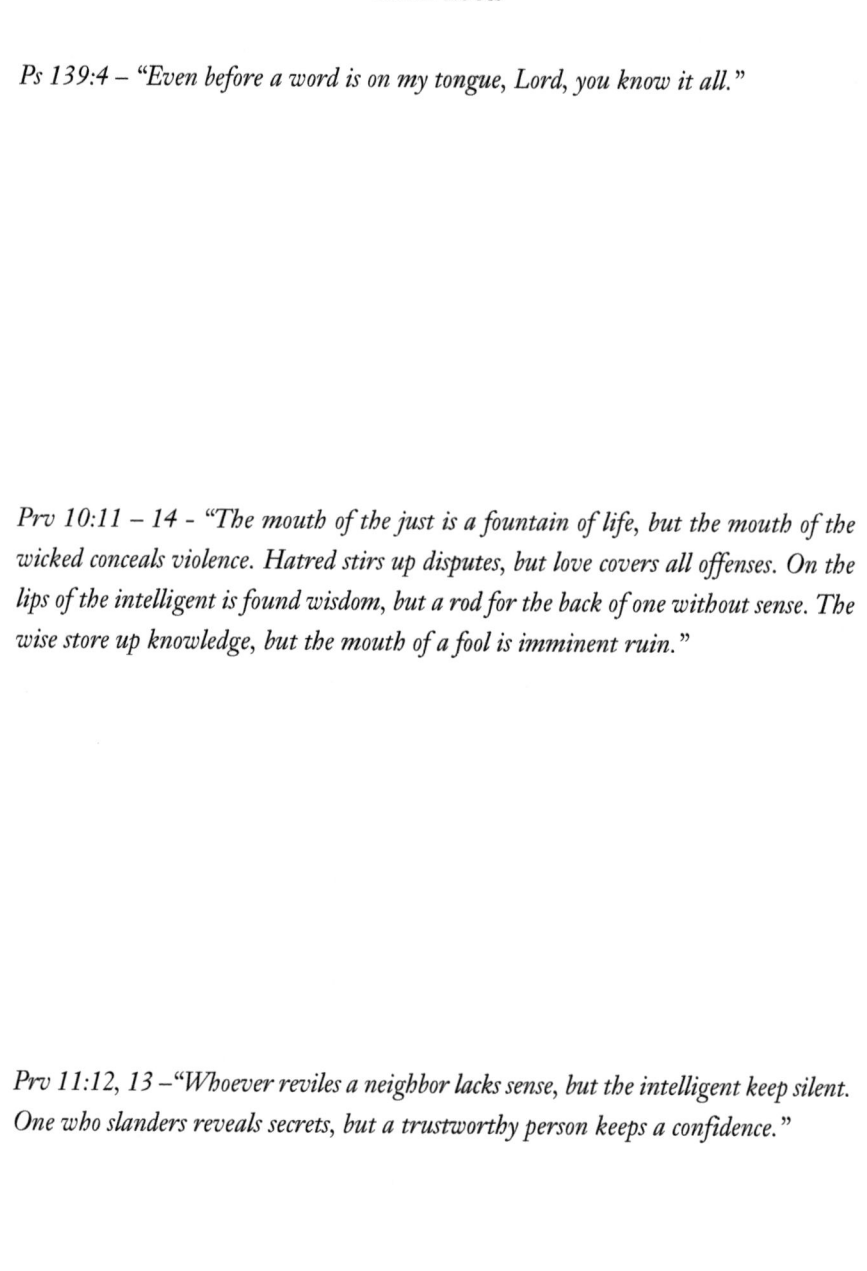

*Ps 139:4* – *"Even before a word is on my tongue, Lord, you know it all."*

*Prv 10:11 – 14* - *"The mouth of the just is a fountain of life, but the mouth of the wicked conceals violence. Hatred stirs up disputes, but love covers all offenses. On the lips of the intelligent is found wisdom, but a rod for the back of one without sense. The wise store up knowledge, but the mouth of a fool is imminent ruin."*

*Prv 11:12, 13* –*"Whoever reviles a neighbor lacks sense, but the intelligent keep silent. One who slanders reveals secrets, but a trustworthy person keeps a confidence."*

# A Three-Ply Cord

*Prv 12:13, 14, 17 – 19, 22, 23; Prv 13;2, 3, 5, 13, 17*
*Wicked speech*
*By the sins of their lips the wicked are ensnared;,,,*
*The babble of some people is like sword thrusts,…*
*Lying lips are an abomination to the Lord,…*
*…the hearts of fools proclaim folly.*
*…from the throat of the treacherous comes violence.*
*…those who open wide their lips bring ruin.*
*…the wicked are odious and disgraceful.*
*Whoever despises the word must pay for it…*
*The wicked messenger brings on disaster,…*

*Blessed speech*
*…the just escape from a tight spot.*
*From the fruit of their mouths people have their fill of good, and the works of their hands come back upon them.*
*Whoever speaks honestly testifies truly,…*
*…the tongue of the wise is healing.*
*Truthful lips endure forever,…*
*Those who are truthful are (the Lord's) delight.*
*From the fruit of the mouth one enjoys good things…*
*Those who guard their mouths preserve themselves,…*
*The just hate deceitful words,…*
*…whoever reveres the command will be rewarded.*
*…a trustworthy envoy is a healing remedy.*

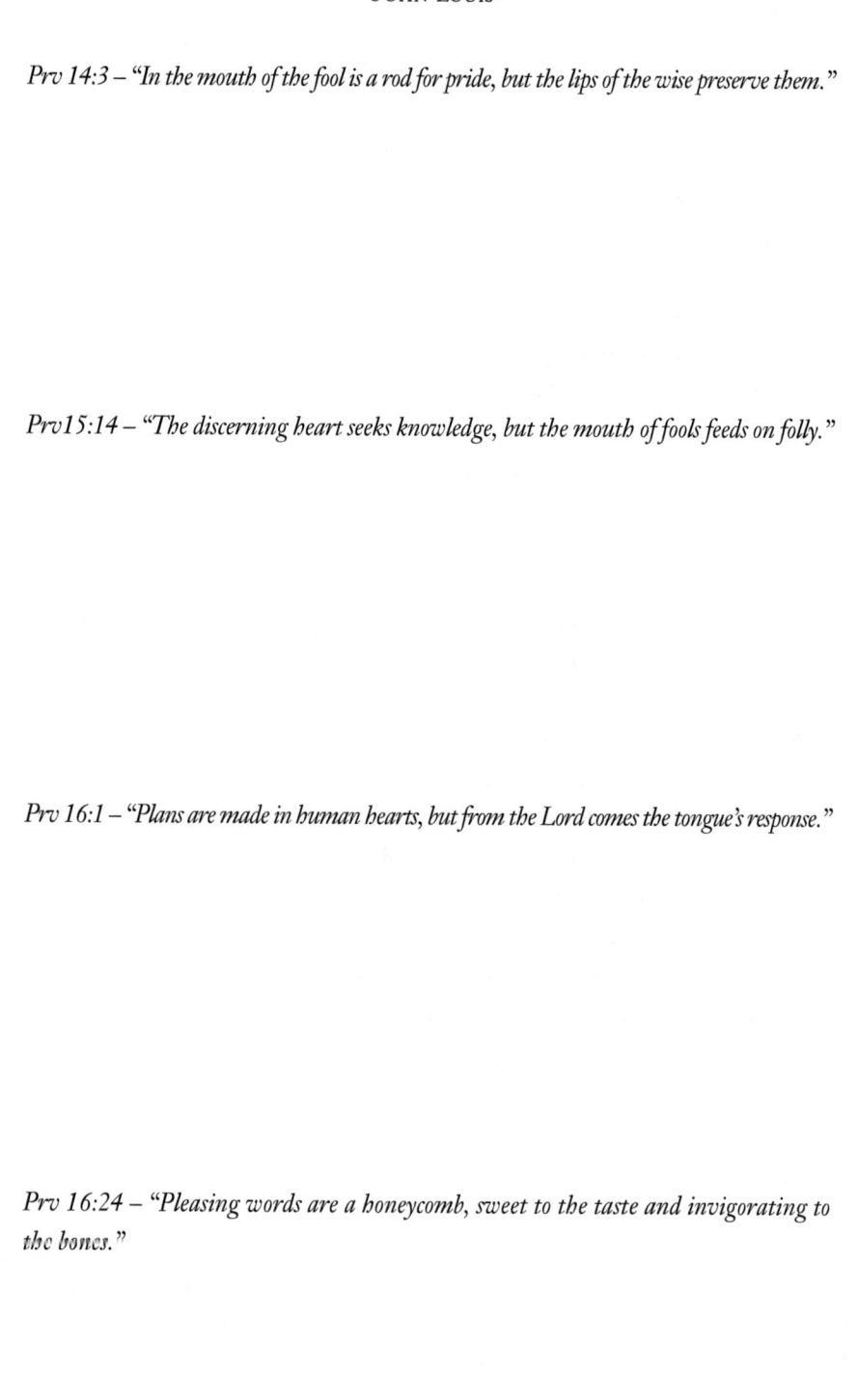

*Prv 14:3* – *"In the mouth of the fool is a rod for pride, but the lips of the wise preserve them."*

*Prv 15:14* – *"The discerning heart seeks knowledge, but the mouth of fools feeds on folly."*

*Prv 16:1* – *"Plans are made in human hearts, but from the Lord comes the tongue's response."*

*Prv 16:24* – *"Pleasing words are a honeycomb, sweet to the taste and invigorating to the bones."*

*Prv 17:7 – 10, 14* - "*Fine words ill fit a fool; how much more lying lips, a noble? A bribe seems a charm to its user; at ever turn it brings success. Whoever overlooks a n offense fosters friendship, but whoever gossips about it separates friends. A single reprimand does more for a discerning person than a hundred lashes for a fool. The start of strife is like the opening of a dam; check a quarrel before it bursts fourth!*

*Prv 20:15 – One can put on gold and abundant jewels, but wise lips are the most precious ornament."*

*Prv 21:23 – Those who guard mouth and tongue guard themselves from trouble."*

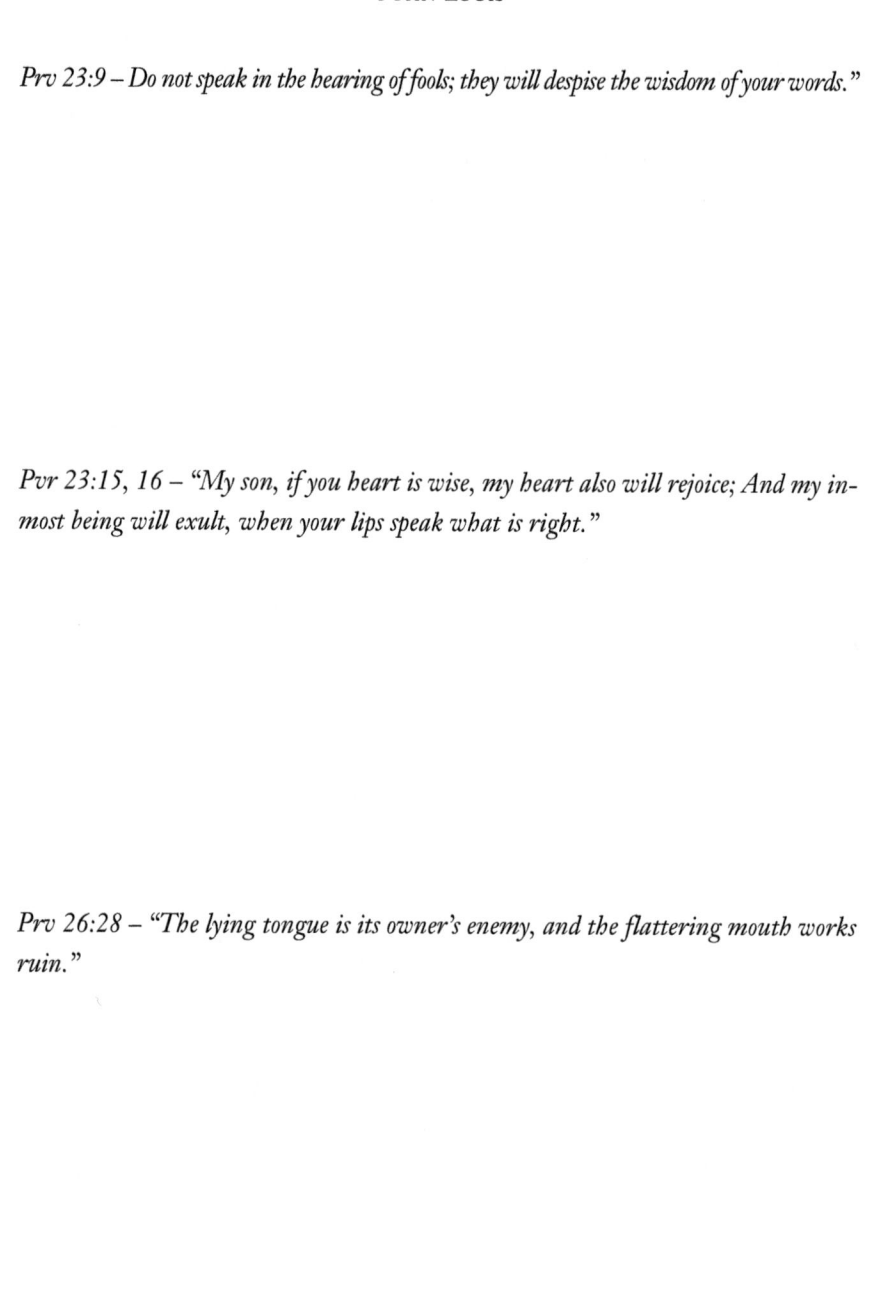

*Prv 23:9* – Do not speak in the hearing of fools; they will despise the wisdom of your words."

*Pvr 23:15, 16* – "My son, if you heart is wise, my heart also will rejoice; And my inmost being will exult, when your lips speak what is right."

*Prv 26:28* – "The lying tongue is its owner's enemy, and the flattering mouth works ruin."

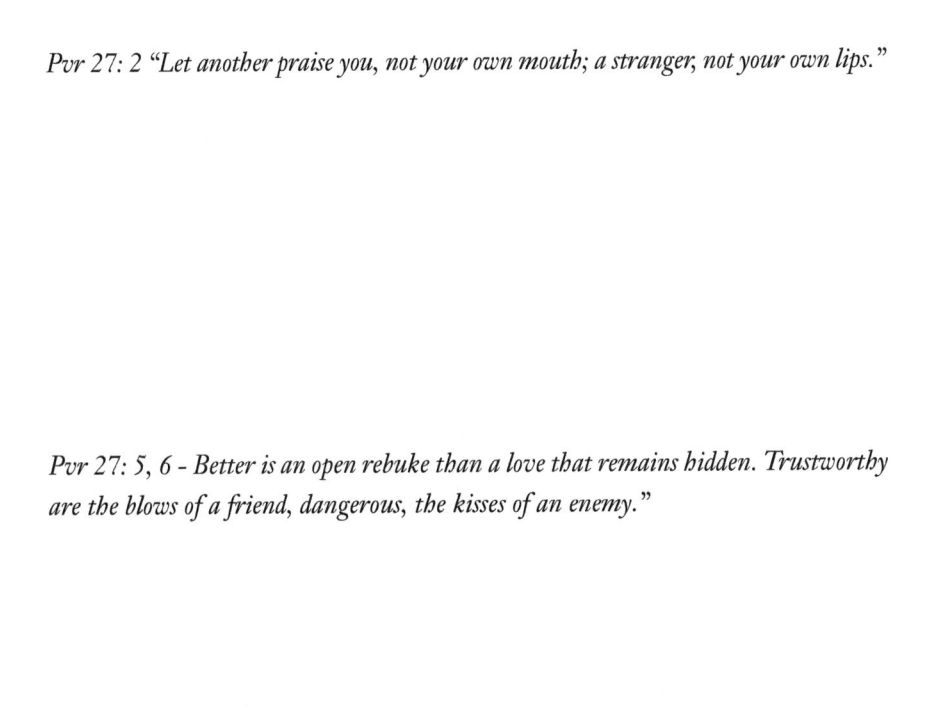

*Pvr 27: 2 "Let another praise you, not your own mouth; a stranger, not your own lips."*

*Pvr 27: 5, 6 - Better is an open rebuke than a love that remains hidden. Trustworthy are the blows of a friend, dangerous, the kisses of an enemy."*

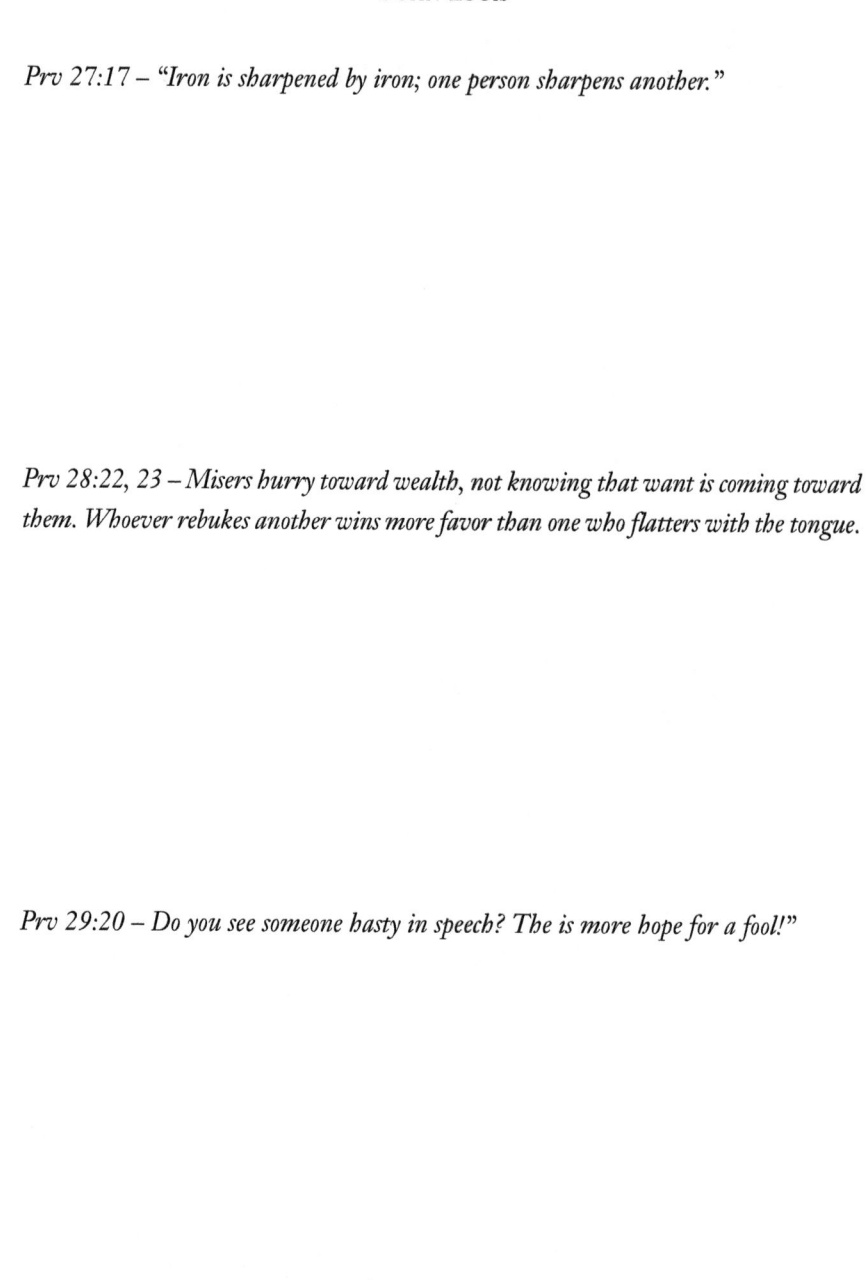

*Prv 27:17* – *"Iron is sharpened by iron; one person sharpens another."*

*Prv 28:22, 23* – *Misers hurry toward wealth, not knowing that want is coming toward them. Whoever rebukes another wins more favor than one who flatters with the tongue.*

*Prv 29:20* – *Do you see someone hasty in speech? The is more hope for a fool!"*

*Prv 30:8* – *"Put falsehood and lying far from me…*

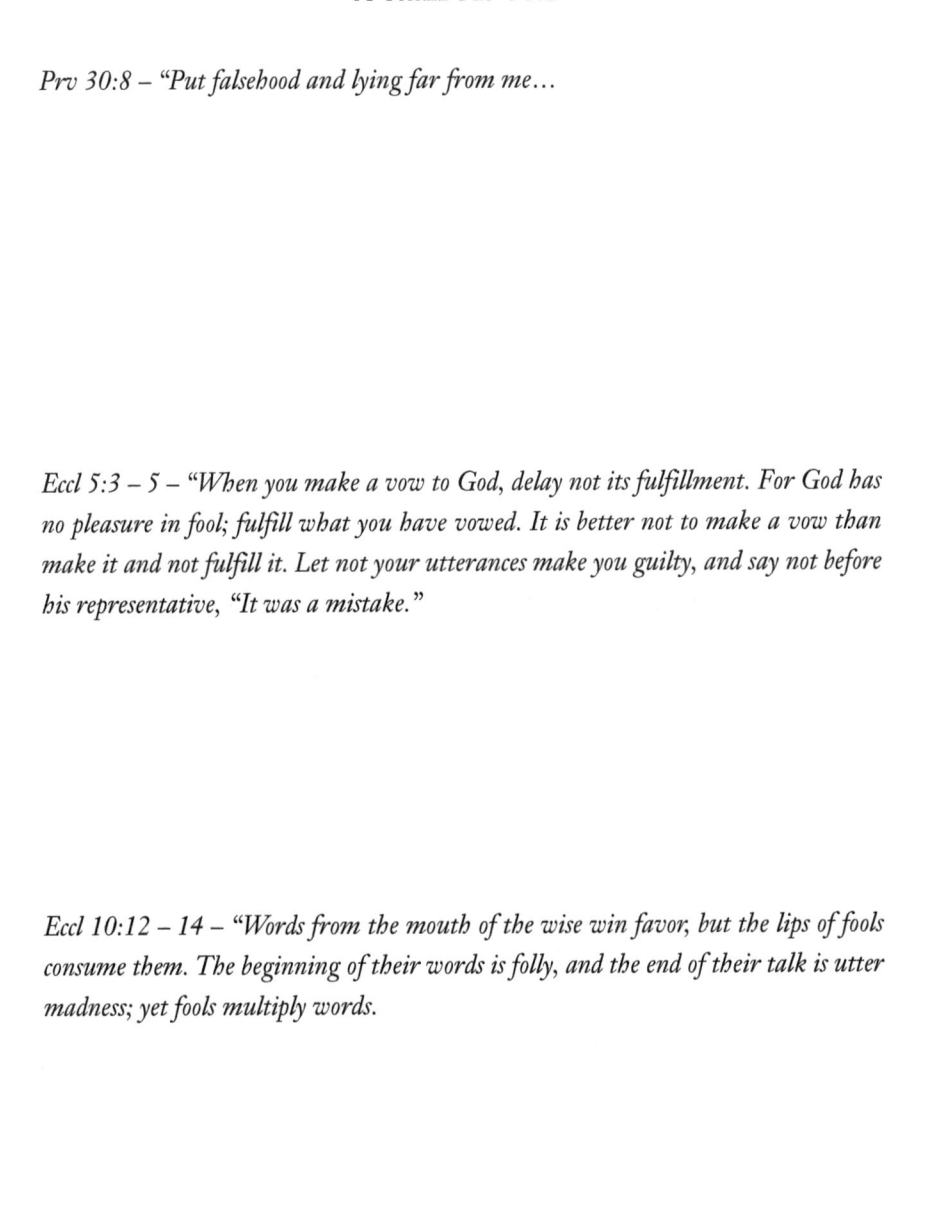

*Eccl 5:3 – 5* – *"When you make a vow to God, delay not its fulfillment. For God has no pleasure in fool; fulfill what you have vowed. It is better not to make a vow than make it and not fulfill it. Let not your utterances make you guilty, and say not before his representative, "It was a mistake."*

*Eccl 10:12 – 14* – *"Words from the mouth of the wise win favor, but the lips of fools consume them. The beginning of their words is folly, and the end of their talk is utter madness; yet fools multiply words.*

*Wis 4:23 – 25, 29 –* "*Do not refrain from speaking at the proper time, and do not hide your wisdom; For wisdom becomes known through speech, and knowledge through the tongue's response. Never speak against the truth. Do not be haughty in your speech.*"

*Wis 5:10 – 15 – Be steadfast regarding your knowledge, and let your speech be consistent. Be swift to hear, but slow to answer. If you can, answer your neighbor; if not, place your hand over your mouth! Honor and dishonor through speaking! The tongue can be your downfall. Do not be called double-tongued. In little or in much, do not act corruptly.*

*Sir 6:1, 5, 6* – *"A bad name, disgrace, and dishonor you will inherit. Thus the wicked, the double-tongued! Pleasant speech multiplies friends, and gracious lips, friendly greetings. Let those who are friendly to you be many, but one in a thousand your confidant.*

*Sir 7:13* – *"Refuse to tell lie after lie, for it never results in good."*

*Sir 8:3, 6, 7* – "*Do not quarrel with loud-mouths, or heap wood upon an open fire. Do not insult one who is old, …Do not rejoice when someone dies;…*"

*Sir 9:17, 18* – "*…the people's leader is proved wise by his words. Loud mouths are feared in their city, and whoever is reckless in speech is hated.*"

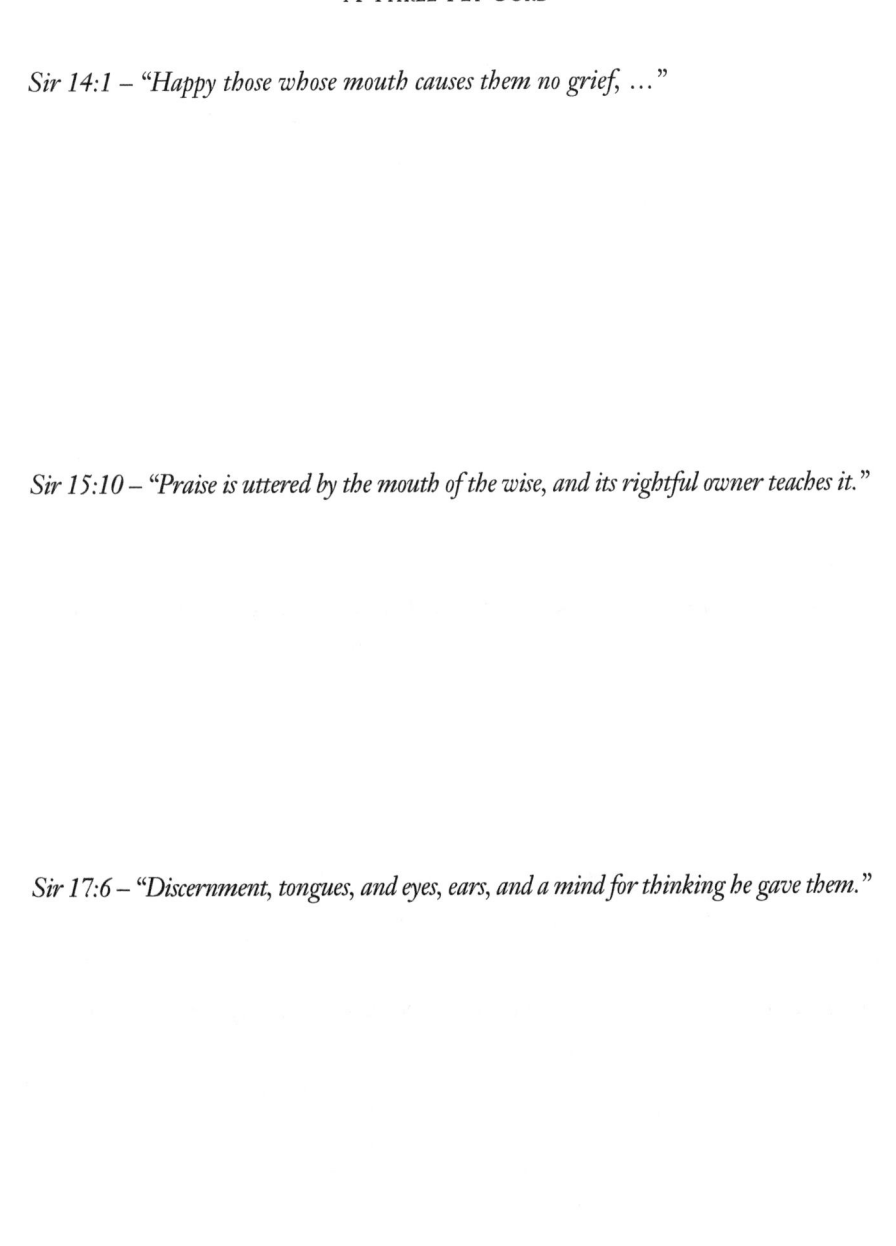

*Sir 14:1* – *"Happy those whose mouth causes them no grief, …"*

*Sir 15:10* – *"Praise is uttered by the mouth of the wise, and its rightful owner teaches it."*

*Sir 17:6* – *"Discernment, tongues, and eyes, ears, and a mind for thinking he gave them."*

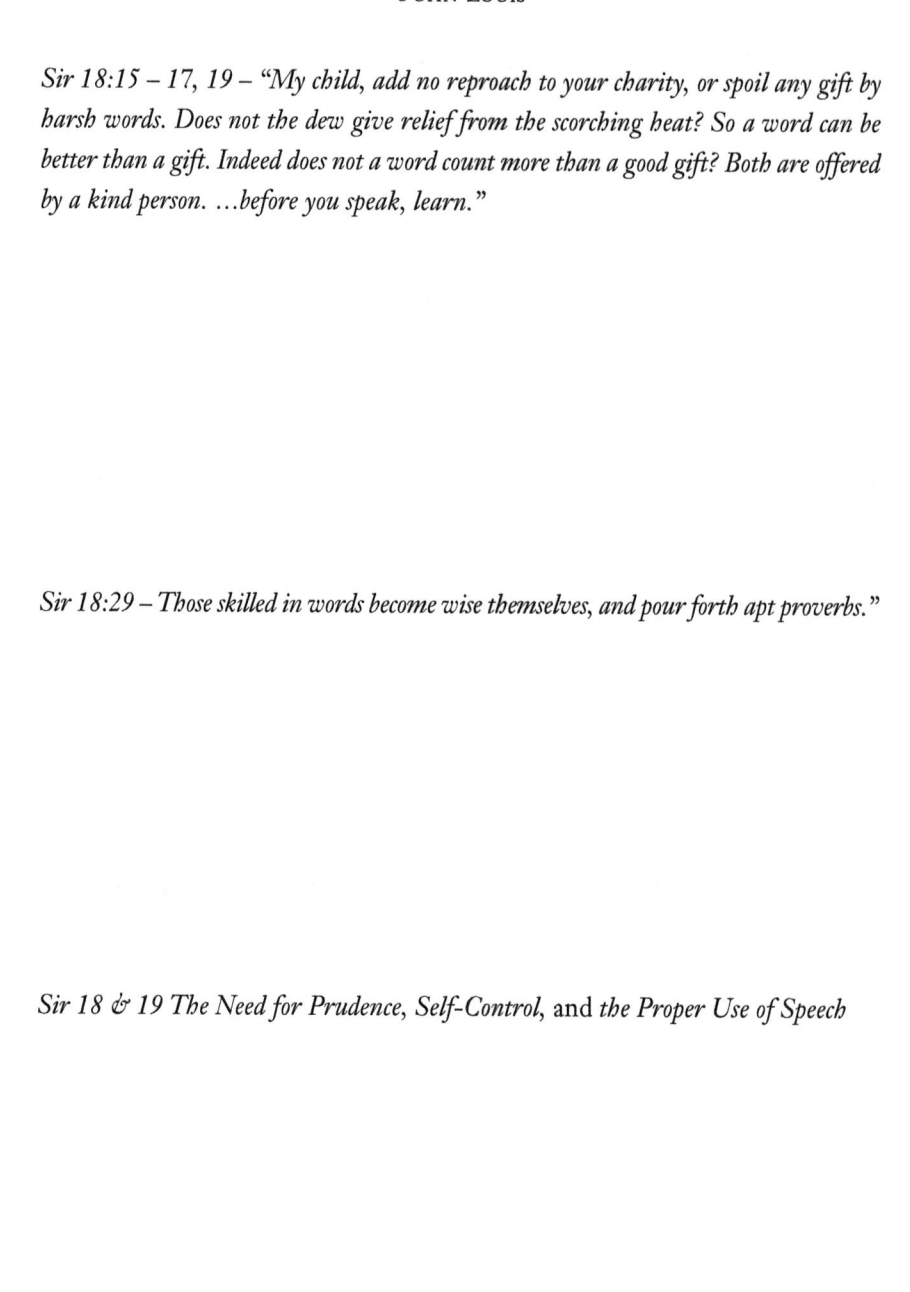

*Sir 18:15 – 17, 19* – *"My child, add no reproach to your charity, or spoil any gift by harsh words. Does not the dew give relief from the scorching heat? So a word can be better than a gift. Indeed does not a word count more than a good gift? Both are offered by a kind person. ...before you speak, learn."*

*Sir 18:29 – Those skilled in words become wise themselves, and pour forth apt proverbs."*

*Sir 18 & 19 The Need for Prudence, Self-Control,* and *the Proper Use of Speech*

*Sir 20:1, 4-8, 18 – There is an admonition that is untimely, but the silent person is the wise one. One is silent and is thought wise; another, for being talkative, is disliked. One is silent, having nothing to say; another is silent, biding his time. The wise remain silent till the right time comes, but a boasting fool misses the proper time. Whoever talks too much is detested;…"*

*Sir 21:16, 20, 25 – 28*
"*A fool's chatter is like a load on a journey, but delight is to be found on the lips of the intelligent.*"
"*Fools raise their voice in laughter, but the prudent at most smile quietly.*"
*The lips of the arrogant talk of what is not their concern, but the discreet carefully weigh their words. The mind of fools is in their mouths, but the mouth of the wise is in their mind. When the godless curse their adversary, they really curse themselves. Slanderers sully themselves, and are hated by their neighbors."*

*Sir 22:6, 10, 13, 22*

*"Like music at the time of mourning is ill timed talk,..."*

*"Whoever talks with a fool talks to someone asleep; when it is over, he says, "What was that?"*

*"Do not talk much with the stupid, or visit the unintelligent."*

*Sir 22:22, 27*
"Should you open your mouth against a friend, do not worry, for you can be reconciled. But a contemptuous insult, a confidence broken, or a treacherous attack will drive any friend away."
"Who will set a guard over my mouth, an effective seal on my lips, That I may not fail through them, and my tongue may not destroy me?"

*Sir 23:7 – 15 Proper Use of the Tongue (consideration of the Second Commandment)*
"*Listen, my children, to instruction concerning the mouth, for whoever keeps it will not be ensnared.*
*Through the lips the sinner is caught, by them the reviler and the arrogant are tripped up. Do not accustom your mouth to oaths, or habitually utter the Holy Name.*
*Just as a servant constantly under scrutiny will not be without bruises, So one who swears continually by the Holy Name will never remain free from sin.*
*Those who swear many oaths heap up offenses; and the scourge will never be far from their houses. If they swear in error, guilt is incurred; if they neglect their obligations, the sin is doubly great. If they swear without reason they cannot be declared innocent, from their households will be filled with calamities.*
*There are words comparable to death; may they never be heard in the inheritance of Jacob. To the devout all such words are foreign; they do not wallow in sin.*
*Do not accustom your mouth to coarse talk, for it involves sinful speech.*
*Keep your father and mother in mind when you sit among the mighty, Lest you forget yourself in their presence and disgrace your upbringing. Then you will wish you had never been born and will curse the day of your birth.*
*Those accustomed to using abusive language will never acquire discipline as long as they live.*"

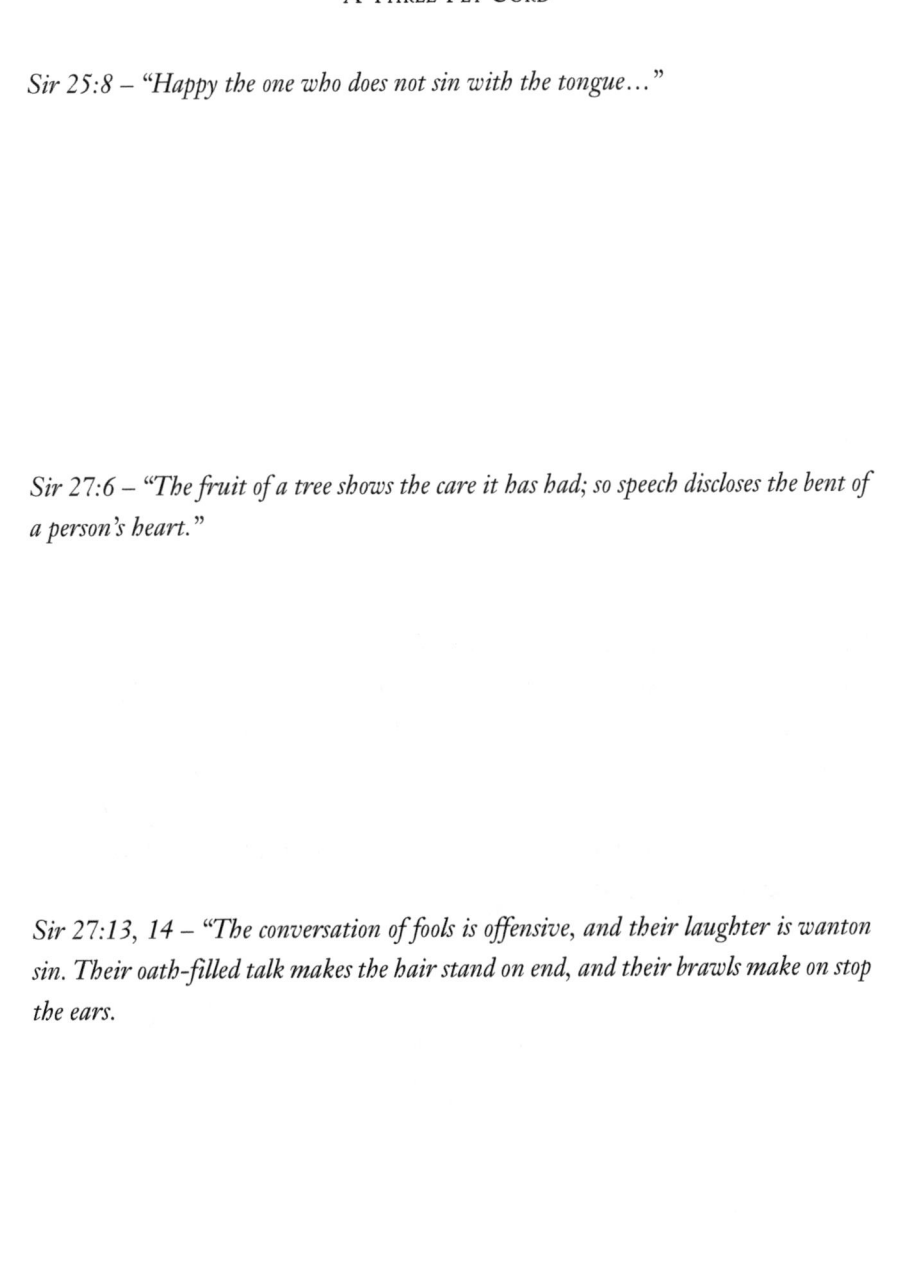

*Sir 25:8* – "*Happy the one who does not sin with the tongue…*"

*Sir 27:6* – "*The fruit of a tree shows the care it has had; so speech discloses the bent of a person's heart.*"

*Sir 27:13, 14* – "*The conversation of fools is offensive, and their laughter is wanton sin. Their oath-filled talk makes the hair stand on end, and their brawls make on stop the ears.*

*Sir 28: 12 – 36 The Evil Tongue*
These twenty-four verses go beyond the caution of chapter twenty-three to discuss the intentional pains caused by using speech to create discord. These cautions detail how death is dealt to the good of creation by poor speech. Please take time to open your bible for contemplation.

*Sir 32:7 – 13* – "Speak, young man, only when necessary, when they have asked you more than once. Be brief, say much in a few words; be knowledgeable and yet quiet. When among elders do not be forward, and with officials do not be too insistent. The lightning that flashes before a hailstorm: the esteem that shines on modesty. Leave in good time and do not be the last; go home quickly without delay. There enjoy doing as you wish, but do not sin through words of pride. Above all, bless your Maker, who showers his favors upon you"

*Sir 33:4* – *"Prepare your words and then you will be listened to; draw upon your training, and give your answer."*

*Sir 37:16, 20* – *"A word is the source of every deed, a thought, of every act."*
*"One may be wise, but if his words are rejected, he will be deprived of all enjoyment."*

*Sir 40:21* – *Flute and harp offer sweet melody, but better than either, a pure tongue."*

*Is 29:13* – "*Since this people draws near with words only and honors me with their lips alone, though their hearts are far from me, and fear of me has become mere precept of human teaching,*"

*Zec 8:16* "*These then are the things you must do: Speak the truth to one another; judge with honesty and complete justice in your gates. Let none of you plot evil against another in your heart, no love a false oath. For all these things I hate – oracle of the Lord.*"

# The New Testament Scriptures

*Mt 5:33 – 37 "Again you have heard that it was said to your ancestors, 'Do not take a false oath, but make good to the Lord all that you vow. But I say to you, do not swear at all: not by heaven, for it is God's throne; not by the earth, for it is his footstool; nor by Jerusalem, for it is the city of the great King. Do not swear by your head, for you cannot make a single hair white or black. Lt you r 'Yes' mean 'Yes,' and your 'No' mean 'No.' Anything more is from the evil one.*

*Mt 12:31, 32 - Therefore, I say to you, every sin and blasphemy will be forgiven people, but blasphemy against the Spirit will not be forgiven. And whoever speaks a word against the Son of Man will be forgiven; but whoever speaks against the holy Spirit will not be forgiven, either in this age or in the age to come.*

*Mt. 12:33 – 37 – "Either declare the tree good and its fruit is good, or declare the tree rotten and its fruit is rotten, for a tree is known by its fruit. You brood of vipers, how can you say good things when you are evil? From the fullness of the heart the mouth speaks. A good person brings forth good out of a store of goodness, but an evil person brings forth evil out of a store of evil. I tell you, on the day of judgment people will render an account for every careless word they speak. By your words you will be acquitted, and by your words you will be condemned.*

*Mt 15:10, 11, 17 – 19 –* "*He summoned the crowd and said to them, "Hear and understand. It is not what enters one's mouth that defiles that person; but what comes out of the mouth is what defiles one. Do you not realize that everything that enters the mouth passes into the stomach and is expelled into the latrine? But the things that come out of the mouth come from the heart, and they defile. For from the heart come evil thoughts, murder, adultery, unchastity, theft, false witness, blasphemy. These are what defile a person, …*"

*Mk 11: 12 – 14 Jesus Curses a Fig Tree*
*The next day as the were leaving Bethany he was hungry. Seeing from a distance a fig tree in leaf, he went over to see if he could find anything on it. When he reached it he found nothing but leaves; it was not the time for figs. And he said to it in reply, "May no one ever eat of your fruit again?" And his disciples heard it."*

*11:20 – 22 The Withered Fig Tree*
*Early in the morning, as they were walking along, they saw the fig tree withered to its roots. Peter remembered and said to him, "Rabbi, look! The fig tree that you cursed has withered." Jesus said to them in reply, "Have faith in God. Amen, I say to you, whoever says to this mountain, 'Be lifted up and thrown into the sea,' and does not doubt in his heart but believes that what he says will happen, it shall be done for him*

*Mk 13:11 "…do not worry beforehand about what you are to say. But say whatever will be given to you at that hour. For it will not be you who are speaking but the holy Spirit.*

*Lk 13:1 – 4 – The Lord's Prayer*
*He was praying in a certain place, and when he had finished, one of his disciples said to him, "Lord, teach us to pray just as John taught his disciples." He said to them, "When you pray, say: Father, hallowed be your name, your kingdom come. Give us each day our daily bread and forgive us our sins for we ourselves forgive everyone in det to us, and do not subject us to the test."*

*Rom 10:8* "*The word is near you, in your mouth and in your heart.*"

*Eph 4:25, 29, 31*
"*Therefore, putting away falsehood, speak the truth, each one to his neighbor, for we are members one of another.*"
"*No foul language should come out of your mouths, but only such as is good for needed edification, that it may impart grace to those who hear.?*
"*All bitterness, fury, anger, shouting, and reviling must be removed from you, along with all malice.*

*Eph 5:3, 4, 17 – 20*

"*Immorality or any impurity or greed must not even be mentioned among you, as is fitting among holy ones, no obscenity or silly or suggestive talk, which is out of place, but instead, thanksgiving.*"

"*Therefore,…try to understand what is the will of the Lord. …be filled with the Spirit, addressing one another [in] psalms and hymns and spiritual songs, singing and playing to the Lord in your hearts, given thanks always for everything in the name of our Lord Jesus Christ to God the Father.*

*1 Tim 4:12* – "*…set an example for those who believe, in speech, conduct, love, faith, and purity."*

*1 Tim 6:20, 21 - …guard what has been entrusted to you. Avoid profane babbling and the absurdities of so-called knowledge. By professing it, some people have deviated from the faith."*

*2 Tim 2:16 - "Avoid profane, idle talk…"*

*Jas 3:2, 5, 6, 8 – 11 Power of the Tongue*

*"If anyone does not fall short in speech, he is a perfect man."*

*"…the tongue is a small member and yet has great pretensions."*

*"The tongue is also fire. It exists among our members as a world of malice, defiling the whole body and setting the entire course of our lives on fire, itself set on fire by Gehenna."*

*"…no human can tame the tongue. It is a restless evil, full of deadly poison. With it we bless the Lord and Father, and with it we curse human beings who are made in the likeness of God. From the same mouth come blessing and cursing. This need not be so, my brothers. Does a spring gush forth from the same opening both pure and brackish water?"*

*Jas 4:15, 16 –* "*…you should say, "If the Lord wills it, we shall live to do this or that. But now you are boasting in your arrogance."*

*1 Pt 3:10* – "*...Keep the tongue from evil and the lips from speaking deceit...*"
Peter is quoting Psalm thirty-four, demonstrating the continuity of scripture through time as a guide for proper living.

# Healing the Wounds of the Embodied Spirit

All three parts of our embodied spirits suffer injury and pain. A physical injury causes hurt to radiate throughout the body. It distracts us from other senses, may overtake another wound, or be so severe as to render us unconsciousness. When the pain reaches our threshold for bearing it, our minds get confused. A hard bump on the head disorients and creates dizziness. We lose our balance and we fall. Now the injury is compounded as both mind and body are hurt.

The conscience, that intersection of mind and spirit, realizes a decision goes against a disciplined principle. We did something we knew was wrong or not certain was right. Such decisions lead to others that may (or may not) lead to further tainted or confusing decisions. Our mind recognizes our dysphoria. The body suffers illness from it. Imperfect behavior becomes habit. Imperfect habit is taught, passed to the next generation. This is the original sin of man passed from generation to generation.

Once hurt, one injury follows another. We need to be healed. Jesus asked in Luke's account, "Which is easier to say, 'Your sins are forgiven?' or to say, 'Rise and walk'?" (Lk 5:23). He already knew that healing the body and the spirit was needed. Decisions in our marriages are not always the right and just decisions. We hurt ourselves and others, and others hurt us. We need healing, and we need healing often. We need to forgive and never let the sun go down on an injury of any kind.

There are times when the injuries between spouses are deliberate and intended to harm. The vows are broken and need to be remade. The vows are sometimes broken, and no matter the effort of one seeking to mend and uphold, the other may have no such inclination to mend at the moment, in a day, or over months or years. Healing can happen in moments. It may also take many long years.

Moreover, it may be that healing is not something that makes whole what is broken, or that suffering pain is a necessary component of healing as in a bodily wound. "Three times I begged the Lord about this, that it might leave me, but he said to me, 'My grace is sufficient for you, for power is made perfect in weakness' " (2 Cor 12:8, 9). Always remember, God walks with you, sometimes may even carry you. His efforts become visible in the advice and counsel of others who are committed to the same ideals of covenant, beginning with your priest, and continuing with well-chosen friends, family members, and/or professionals.

These counselors must be like-minded in their commitment to the concepts of covenant, someone who will walk the healing journey with you. A confidant will reflect to you with honesty according to covenant principle. They will support you in making right and just decisions and caution you when thoughts turn from Truth. The journey to healing any wound, especially to a marriage vow, is a difficult one. It is an emotional one, and you will be sharing some of your deepest emotions. The confidant should have the same goal in mind as you do, to help heal the wound and restore the actions toward fulfilling the marriage vows.

Choose counselors carefully. Likely, you have cultivated solid friendships and will already have those who support covenant commitment. Witnesses chosen for your wedding party should already be these people. Be careful with your choices. Would you choose a foot doctor to set a broken collarbone? Would you select a landscaper to repair your roof? Why ask the advice of a person on their second or third contract marriage how to heal your covenant marriage vow? A professional counselor may be helpful with a mental struggle and a lawyer well trained in the art of the courts. Both are well and good choices for help in discussing social constructs of marriage. One whose first recommendation is divorce does not understand covenant. Choose another.

"Therefore, confess your sins to one another and pray for one another, that you may be healed. The fervent prayer of a righteous person is very powerful"

(Jas 5:16). These counselors should be someone who would pray with you and for you. Also, look for someone who is of the same gender. Your emotions will cloud your judgment, so you want a companion. Do not pick a companion you might transfer your feelings to if you want to heal your covenant vows.

Once healing begins, the wounds must be recognized and tended to. They will heal in time, yet scars may remain. Those may be scratched or torn open throughout the process. We have come to understand the metaphor of 'that old athletic injury' and the difficulties of 'tennis elbow' *which flare up from time-to-time*. We must also come to understand the continued annoyances, frequent or infrequent, of the injuries to our marriages. Our prayer is that the deep healing continues to be effective so when those distractions arise they are minimized and may be overcome

Again, remember you are not alone. Always remember that the sacramental, covenant wedding vows bind three persons; husband, wife, and God. God's love is the permanent balm for binding and healing in marriage. The hand of Christ will be there in the person of the priest and trusted counselors. I pray you are open and receive the grace and peace you need to be healed in your mind, body, and spirit that through this work you may take the next steps toward healing your covenant and continuing on your journey with your spouse.

Grace and peace of God our Father, the presence of our Lord, Jesus Christ, and the fellowship of the Holy Spirit be with you and heal you, that you may continue to honor your covenant marriage.

# The First Covenant Scriptures

*Genesis 20: 17 "Abraham then interceded with God and God restored health to Abimelech, to his wife, and his maidservants, so that they bore children;"*

1Kgs17:17, 20 – 22 *"Some time later the son of the woman (he was staying with) fell sick, and his sickness grew more severe until he stopped breathing. (Elijah) called out to the Lord: "Lord, my God, will you afflict even the widow with whom I am staying by killing her son?" Then he stretched himself out upon the child three times and he called out to the Lord: "Lord, my God, let the life breath return to the body of this child." The Lord heard the prayer of Elijah: the life breath returned to the child's body and he lived."*

*2 Kgs 4:32 – 37 – When Elisha reached the house, he found the boy dead, lying on the bed. He went in, closed the door on them both, and prayed to the Lord. Then he lay upon the child on the bed, placing his mouth upon the child's mouth, placing his eyes upon the eyes, and hands upon the hands. As Elisha stretched himself out upon over child, the boy's flesh became warm. He arose, paced up and down the room, then once more stretched himself over him, and the boy sneezed seven times and opened his eyes. "…Call the (mother)…and Elisha said, "Take your son."*

*2 Kgs 39 – 41 – Someone went out into the field to gather herbs and found a wild vine, from which he picked a sack full of poisonous wild gourds. On his return he cut them up into the port of vegetable stew without anybody's knowing it. The stew was served, but when they began. To eat it, they cried, "Man of God, there is death in the pot!" And they could not eat it. He said, "Bring some meal." He threw it into the pot and said, "Serve it to the people to eat." And there was no longer anything harmful in the pot."*

*2 Kgs 5:9 – 14 –* "*Naaman came with his horses and chariot and stopped at the door of Elisha's house. Elisha sent him the message; "Go and wash seven times in the Jordan, and your flesh will heal, and you will be clean." But Naaman went away angry, saying, "I thought that he would surely come out to me and stand there to call on the name of the Lord his God and would move his hand over the place, and thus cure the leprous spot. Are not the rivers of Damascus, the Abana and the Pharpar, better than all the waters of Israel? Could I not wash in them and be cleansed? With this, he turned about in anger and left. But his servants came up and reasoned with him: "My father, if the prophet told you to do something extraordinary, would you not do it? All the more since he told you, "Wash, and be clean?" So Naaman went down and plunged into the Jordan seven times, according to the word of the man of God. His flesh became again like the flesh of a little child, and he was clean."*

*2 Kgs 20:5, 6* – *"...Thus says the Lord, the God of David your father: I have heard your prayer; I have seen your tears. Now I am healing you. On the third day you shall go up to the house of the Lord. I will add to your life fifteen years. I will rescue you and this city from the hand of the king of Assyria; I will be a shield to this city for my own sake and the sake of David my servant."*

*Jb 5:17 – 19* – *"Happy the one whom God reprove! The Almighty's discipline do not reject. For he wounds, but he binds up; he strikes, but his hands give healing. Out of six troubles he will deliver you, and at the seventh no evil shall touch you.*

*Jb 8:5, 6* – *"Still, if you yourself have recourse to God and make supplication to the Almighty, Should you be blameless and upright, surely now he will rouse himself for you and restore your rightful home."*

*Jb 22:21 – 25* – *"Settle with Him and have peace. That way good shall come to you: Receive instruction from his mouth, and place His words in your heart. If you return to the Almighty, you will be restored;…"*

*Jb. 22:30* – *"He will deliver whoever is innocent; you shall be delivered if your hands are clean."*

*Ps 5:3, 4 – Attend to the sound of my cry, my king and my God? For to you I will pray, Lord; in the morning you will hear my voice; in the morning I will plead before you and wait."*

*Ps 6:3 – 5 –* "*Have pity on me, Lord, for I am weak; heal me, Lord, for my bones are shuddering. My soul too is shuddering greatly – and you Lord, How long...? Turn back, Lord, rescue my soul; save me because of your mercy."*

*Ps 20 Prayer for the King in Time of War*

I. *The Lord answer you in time of distress; the name of the God of Jacob defend you! May he send you help from the sanctuary, from Zion be your support. May he remember your every offering, graciously accept your burnt offering.*

*Grant what is in your heart, fulfill your every plan. May we shout for joy at your victory, raise the banners in the name of our God. The Lord grant your every petition!*

II. *Now I know the Lord gives victory to his anointed. He will answer him from the holy heavens with a strong arm that brings victory. Some rely on chariots, others on horses, but we on the name of the Lord our God. They collapse and fall, but we stand strong and firm. Lord, grant victory to the king; answer when we call upon you.*

*Ps 30 Thanksgiving for Deliverance*

I. I praise you, Lord, for you raised me up and didn't let my enemies rejoice over me. O Lord, my God, I cried out to you for help and you healed me. Lord, you brought my soul up from Sheol; you let me live, from going down to the pit.

II. Sing praise to the Lord, you faithful; give thanks to his holy memory. For his anger lasts but a moment; his favor a lifetime. At dusk weeping comes for the night; but at dawn there is rejoicing.

III. Complacent, I once said, I shall never be shaken. Lord, you showed me favor established for me mountains of virtue. But when you hid your face I was struck with terror. To you, Lord, I cried out; with the Lord I pleaded for mercy; What gain is there from my lifeblood, from my going down to the grave? Does dust give you thanks or declare your faithfulness? Hear, O Lord, have mercy on me; Lord, be my helper.

IV. You changed my mourning into dancing; you took off my sackcloth and clothed me with gladness. So that my glory may praise you and not be silent. O Lord, my God, forever will I give you thanks.

*Ps 41 Thanksgiving After Sickness*

I. *Blessed the one concerned for the poor; on a day of misfortune, the Lord delivers him. The Lord keeps and preserves him, makes him blessed in the land and does not betray him to his enemies. The Lord sustains him on his sickbed, you turn down his bedding whenever he is ill.*

II. *Even I have said, "Lord, take note of me; heal me, although I have sinned against you. My enemies say bad things against me: 'When will he die and his name be forgotten?' When someone comes to visit me, he speaks without sincerity. His heart stores up malice; when he leaves, he gossips. Al those who hate me whisper together against me; they imagine the worst about me; 'He has had ruin poured over him; that one lying down will never rise again.' Even my trusted friend, who ate my bread, has raised his heel against me.*

III. *But you, Lord, take note of me to raise me up that I may repay them. By this I will know you are pleased with me, that my enemy no longer shouts in triumph over me. In my integrity may you support me and let me stand in your presence forever. Blessed be the Lord, the God of Israel, from all eternity and forever. Amen. Amen.*

*Ps 119:93, 94 – "I will never forget your precepts; through them you give me life. I am yours; save me, for I cherish your precepts."*

*Wis 2:23 – "For God formed us to be imperishable; the image of his own nature he made us."*

*Sir 30:21 – 25 –* "*Do not give in to sadness, or torment yourself deliberately. Gladness of heart is the very life of a person, and cheerfulness prolongs his days. Distract yourself and renew your courage, drive resentment far away from you; For grief has killed many, and nothing is to be gained from resentment. Envy and anger shorten one's days, and anxiety brings on premature old age. Those who are cheerful and merry at table benefit from their food.*"

*Sir 31:20, 22 – Moderate eating ensures sound slumber and a clear mind on rising the next day. Listen to me, my child, and do not scorn me; later you will find my advice good. In whatever you do, be moderate, and no sickness will befall you."*

*Sir 38:1, 2, 4, 6-9, 12 – 14 –*
*"Make friends with the doctor, for he is essential to you; God has also established him in his profession. From God the doctor has wisdom, …God makes the earth yield healing herbs which the prudent should not neglect;*
*He endows people with knowledge, to glory in his mighty works, through which the doctor eases pain, and the druggist prepares his medicines.*

*Thus God's work continues without ceasing in its efficacy on the surface of the earth. My son, when you are ill, do not delay, but pray to God, for it is he who heals.*
*Then, give the doctor his place lest he leave you; you need him too, For there are times when recovery is in his hands. He too prays to God that his diagnosis may be correct and his treatment bring about a cure.*

*Sir 48: 5, 13* – "*You brought a dead body back to life from Sheol, by the will of the Lord. Nothing was beyond his power,...*"

*Is 6:9, 10* "*Go and say to the people, 'Listen carefully, but do not understand! Look intently, but do not perceive! Make the heart of this people sluggish, dull their ears and close their eyes; Lest the see with their eyes, and hear with their ears, and their heart understand, and they turn and be healed'.*"

*Is 35:4 – 6 – "Say to the fearful of heart: Be strong, do not fear! Here is your God, he comes with vindication; With divine recompense he comes to save you. Then the eyes of the blind shall see, and the ears of the deaf be opened; Then the lame shall leap like a stag, and the mute tongue sing for joy.*

*Is 38:16, 17 – Those live whom the Lord protects; yours is the life of my spirit. You have given me health and restored my life! Peace in place of bitterness! You have preserved my life from the pit of destruction; Behind your back you cast all my sins."*

*Jer 17:14 – Heal me, Lord, that I may be healed; save me, that I may be saved, for you are my praise."*

*Jer 30:17 – For I will restore your health; I will heal your injuries – oracle of the Lord."*

*Dn 1:12 – 15 –* "*The Daniel said to the guardian whom the chief chamberlain had put in charge of Danial, Hananiah, Mishael, and Azariah, "Please test your servants for ten days. Let us be given vegetables to eat and whatever to drink. Then see how we look in comparison with the other young men who eat from the royal table, and treat your servants according to what you see" He agreed to this request, and tested them for ten days; after ten days they looked healthier and better fed than any of the young men who ate from the royal table.*"

*Hos 11:4 – "I drew them with human cords, with bands of love; I fostered them like those who raise an infant to their cheeks; I bent down to feed them."*

# Gospel Scriptures Introduction

The writing of the canonical Gospels took place over a relatively short period of time, from about 60 A.D. to 70 A. D. for Mark, Matthew, and Luke. The Gospel of John is thought to be written around 92 A.D. Mark wrote to a persecuted Church, Matthew to a mostly Jewish audience, and Luke to the Gentiles. Mark seems likely to be the first of the books completed. Matthew and Luke draw on Mark, using most of Mark's verses as a framework for their own. Consequently, there is a great deal of overlap. As Luke was a physician, his stories are used to demonstrate Jesus' healing works. The other two synoptic Gospel writers are cross-referenced. The Gospel of John is presented separately.

*Lk 4:33 – 35 –* "*In the synagogue there was a man with the spirit of an unclean demon, and he cried out in a loud voice, "Ha! What have you to do with us, Jesus of Nazareth? Have you come to destroy us? I know who you are – the Holy One of God!" Jesus rebuked him and said, "Be quiet! Come out of him!" Then the demon threw the man down in front of them and came out of him without doing him any harm.*" (Mt 8:29, Mk 1:23-24)

*Lk 4:38, 39 – After he left the synagogue, the entered the house of Simon. Simon's mother-in-law was afflicted with a sever fever, and they interceded with him about her. He stood over her, rebuked the fever, and it left her. She got up immediately and waited on them."*
(Mt 8:14, 15, Mk 1:29 – 31)

Lk 5:12 – 14 – *"Now there was a man full of leprosy in one of the towns where he was; and when he saw Jesus, he fell prostrate, pleaded with him , and said, 'Lord, if you wish, you can make me clean.' Jesus said, ' I do will it. Be made clean.' And the leprosy left him immediately. Then he ordered him not to tell anyone, but 'Go, show yourself to the priest and offer for your cleansing what Moses prescribed;..."*
(Mt 8:2 – 4, Mk 2:6)

*Lk 5:17 – 26 "After this he went out One Day as Jesus was teaching, Pharisees and teachers of the law were sitting there who had come from every village of Galilee and Judea and Jerusalem, and the power of the Lord was with him for healing. And some men brought on a stretcher a man who was paralyzed; they were trying to bring him in because of the crowd, they went up on the roof and lowered him on the stretcher through the tiles into the middle in front of Jesus. When he saw their faith, he said, 'As for you, your sins are forgiven.'"*

"Then the scribes and Pharisees began to ask themselves, 'Who is this who speaks blasphemies? Who but God along can forgive sins?'"

"Jesus knew their thoughts and said to them in reply, 'What are you thinking in your hearts? Which is easier, to say, 'Your sins are forgiven, 'or to say, 'Rise and walk'? But that you may know that the Son of Man has authority on earth to forgive sins' – he said to the man who was paralyzed, 'I say to you, rise, pick up your stretcher, and go home.' He stood up immediately before them, picked up what he had been lying on, and went home, glorifying God."

(Mt 9:1 – 8, Mk 2:1 – 12)

*Lk 6:6, 10* – "One another sabbath he went into the synagogue and taught, and there was a man there whose right hand was withered. – Looking around at them all, he then said to him, 'Stretch out your hand.' He did so and his hand was restored."
(Mt 12:9-14, Mk 3:1-6)

*Lk 6:17, 18* – "And he came down with them and stood on a stretch of level ground. A great crowd of his disciples and a large number of the people from all Judea and Jerusalem and the coastal region of Tyre and Sidon came to hear him and to be healed of their diseases; and even those who were tormented by unclean spirits were cured."
(Mt 4:23 – 25, Mk 3:7 – 10)

Lk 7:1 – 10 – *"...he entered Capernaum. A centurion there had a slave who was ill and about to die, and he was valuable to him. When he heard about Jesus, he sent elders of the Jews to him, asking him to come and save the life of his slave. They approached Jesus and strongly urged him to come, saying, 'He deserves to have you do this for him, for he loves our nation and he build the synagogue for us.' And Jesus went with them, but when he was only a short distance from the house, the centurion sent friends to tell him, 'Lord, do not trouble yourself, for I am not worthy to come to you; but say the word and let my servant be healed. For I too am a person subject to authority, with soldiers subject to me. And I say to one, 'Go, 'and he goes; and to another, 'come here,' and he comes; and to my slave, 'Do this.' and he does it.' When Jesus heard this he was amazed at him and, turning, said to the crown following him, 'I tell you, not even in Israel have I found such faith.' When the messengers returned to the house, they found the slave in good health."*
(Mt 8:5 – 13, Jn 4:43-54)

Lk 7:12-15 – *"As he drew near to the gate of the city, a man who had died was being carried out, the only son of his mother, and she was a widow. A large crowd from the city was with her. When the Lord saw her, he was moved with pity for her and said to her, 'Do not week.' He stepped forward and touched the coffin; at this the bearers halted, and he said, 'Young man, I tell you, arise!'. The dead man sat up and began to speak, and Jesus gave him to his mother."*

*Lk 8:40-42, 49-54* – "*When Jesus returned, the crowd welcomed him, for they were all waiting for him. And a man named Jairus, an official of the synagogue, came forward. He fell at the feet of Jesus and begged him to come to his house, because he had on only daughter, about twelve years old, and she was dying. While he was still speaking, someone from the synagogue official's house arrived and said, 'Your daughter is dead; do not trouble the teacher any longer' On hearing this, Jesus answered them, 'Do not be afraid; just have faith and she will be saved.' When he arrived at the house he allowed no one to enter with him except Peter and John and James, and the child's father and mother. All were weeping and mourning for her, when he said, 'Do not weep any longer, for she is not dead, but sleeping.' And the ridiculed him, because they knew that she was dead. But he took her by the hand and called to her, 'Child, arise!' Her breath returned and she immediately arose.*"
(Mt 9:18-26, Mk 5:21-43)

*Lk 8:43-48* – "*And a woman afflicted with hemorrhages for twelve years, who [had spent her whole livelihood on doctors and] was unable to be cured by anyone, came up behind him and touched the tassel of his cloak. Immediately her bleeding stopped. Jesus then asked, 'Who touched me?' While all were denying it, Peter said, 'Master, the crowds are pushing and pressing in upon you.' But Jesus said, 'Someone has touched me; for I know that power has gone out from me.' When the woman realized that she had not escaped notice, she came forward trembling. Falling down before him, she explained in the presence of all the people why she had touched him and how she had been healed immediately. He said to her, 'Daughter, your faith has saved you; go in peace.'"*
(Mt 9:20-22, Mk 5:25-34)

*Lk 9:1, 2* – "*He summoned the Twelve and gave them power and authority over all demons and to cure diseases, and he sent them to proclaim the kingdom of God and to heal [the sick].*"
(Mt 10:1, 5-15, Mk 6:7-13)

*Lk 9:10, 11* – "*When the apostles returned, they explained to him what they had done. He took them and withdrew in private to a town called Bethsaida. The crowds, meanwhile, learned of this and followed him. He received them and spoke to them about the kingdom of God, and he healed those who needed to be cured.*"
(Mt 14:13-21; Mk 6:30-44)

*Lk 9:38, 40-42* – "*There was a man in the crowd who cried out, 'Teacher, I beg you, look at my son;...I begged your disciples to cast it (a demon) out but they could not.' Jesus said in reply, 'O faithless and perverse generation, how long will I be with you and endure you? Bring your son here.' As he was coming forward, the demon threw him to the ground in a convulsion; but Jesus rebuked the unclean spirit, healed the boy, and returned him to his father.*"
(Mt 17:14-18, Mk 9:14-27)

*Lk 10:8* – *"Whatever town you enter and they welcome you, eat what is set before you, cure the sick in it and say to them, 'The kingdom of God is at hand for you.'"* (Mt 11:25-27)

*Lk 13:10-13* – "*He was teaching in a synagogue on the sabbath. And a woman was there who for eighteen years had been crippled by a spirit; she was bent over, completely incapable of standing erect. When Jesus saw her, he called to her and said, 'Woman, you are set free of your infirmity.' He laid hands on her, and she at once stood up straight, and glorified God.*"

*Lk 14:1, 2, 4* – "*On a sabbath he went to dine at the home of one of the leading Pharisees, and the people there were observing him carefully. In front of him there was a man suffering from dropsy. …so he took the man and, after he had healed him, dismissed him.*"

*Lk 17:12-16* – *"As he was entering a village, ten lepers met [him]. The stood at a distance from him and raised their voice, saying, 'Jesus, Master! Have pity on us!' And when he saw them, he said, 'God show yourselves to the priests.' As they were going they were cleansed. And one of them, realizing he had been healed, returned, glorifying God in a loud voice and he fell at the feet of Jesus and thanked him."*

John Louis

# Healing in the Gospel of John

*Jn 4:46-51 – Then he returned to Cana in Galilee, where he had made the water wine. Now there was a royal official whose son was ill in Capernaum. When he heard that Jesus had arrived in Galilee from Judea, he went to him and asked him to come down and heal his son, who was near death. Jesus said to him, 'Unless you people see signs and wonders, you will not believe.' The royal official said to him, 'Sir, come down before my child dies.' Jesus said to him, 'You may go; you son will live.' The man believed what Jesus said to him and left. While he was on his way back, his slaves met him and told him that this boy would live."*
(Lk 7:1-10)

*Jn 5:2-9* – "*Now there is in Jerusalem at the Sheep [Gate] a pool called in Hebrew Bethesda, with five porticoes. In these lay a large number of ill, blind, lame, and crippled. One man was there who had been ill the thirty-eight years. When Jesus saw him lying there and knew that he had been ill for a long time, he said to him, 'Do you want to be well?' The sick man answered him, 'Sir, I have no one to put me into the pool when the water is stirred up; while I am on my way, someone else gets down there before me.' Jesus said to him, 'Rise, take up your mat, and walk.' Immediately the man became well, took up his mat, and walked.*"

*Jn 9:1, 5-7* – "*As he passed by he saw a man blind from birth. "While I am in the world, I am the light of the world." When he had said this, he spat on the ground and made clay with the saliva, and smeared the clay on his eyes, and said to him 'Go wash in the Pool at Siloam' (which means Sent). So he went and washed, and came back able to see.*"

*Jn 11:38-44* – "So Jesus, perturbed again, came to the tomb. It was a cave, and a stone lay across it. Jesus said,' Take away the stone.' Martha, the dead man's sister, said to him, 'Lord, by now there will be a stench; he has been dead for four days.' Jesus said to her, 'Did I not tell you that if you believe you will see the glory of God?' So they took away the stone. And Jesus raised his eyes and said, 'Father, I thank you for hearing me. I know that you always hear me; but because of the crowd here I have said this, that they may believe that you sent me.' And when he had said this, he cried out in a loud voice, 'Lazarus, come out!' The dead man came out, tied hand and foot with burial bands, and his face was wrapped in a cloth. So Jesus said …, 'Untie him and let him go.'"

The institution of and demonstration of the Sacrament of Reconciliation, a healing Sacrament of the Church.

*Jn 20:22, 23: "And when he had said this, he breathed on them and said to them, "Receive the holy Spirit. Whose sins you forgive are forgiven them, and whose sins you retain are retained."*

*Jn 21:15 – 17, 21: When they had finished breakfast, Jesus said to Simon Peter, "Simon, son of John, do you love me more than these?" he said to him "Yes, Lord, you know that I love you." He said to him, "Feed my lambs." He then said to him a second time, "Simon, son of John, do you love me?" He said to him, "yes, Lord, you know that I love you." He said to him, "Tend my sheep." He said to him a third time, "Simon, son of John, do you love me:" Peter was distressed that he had said to him a third time, "Do you love me?" and he said to him, "Lord, you know everything; you know that I love you." Jesus said to him, "Feed my sheep." And when he had said this, he said to him, "Follow me."*

*Acts 3:5, 6 "Peter said, "I have neither silver nor gold, but what I do have I give you: in the name of Jesus Christ the Nazorean, rise and walk."*

*Acts 5:15, 16 "Thus they even carried the sick out into the streets and laid them on cots and mats so that when Peter came by, at least his shadow might fall on one or another of them. A large number of people from the towns in the vicinity of Jerusalem also gathered, bringing the sick and those disturbed by unclean spirits, and they were all cured."*

*Acts 8:6 – 9 "With one accord, the crowds paid attention to what was said by Philip when they heard it and saw the signs he was doing. For unclean spirits, crying out in a loud voice, came out of many possessed people, and many paralyzed and crippled people were cured. There was great joy in that city."*

*Acts 9:15 – 19 "But the Lord said to him, "Go, for this man is a chosen instrument of mine to carry my name before Gentiles, kings, and Israelites, and I will show him what he will have to suffer for my name." So Ananias went and entered the house; laying his hands on him, he said, "Saul, my brother, the Lord has sent me, Jesus who appeared to you on the way by which you came, that you may regain your sight and be filled with the holy Spirit." Immediately things like scales fell from his eyes and he regained his sight. He got up and was baptized, and when he had eaten, he recovered his strength."*

*Acts 9:33-35* "There he found a man named Aeneas, who had been confined to bed for eight years, for he was paralyzed. Peter said to him, "Aeneas, Jesus Christ heals you. Get up and make your bed." He got up at once. And all the inhabitants of Lydda and Sharon saw him, and they turned to the Lord."

*Acts 9:36 – 42 (abbrev)* "Now in Joppa there was a disciple named Tabitha. She was completely occupied with good deeds and almsgiving. ...she fell sick and died. ...disciples, hearing that Peter was there..."Please come to us without delay. So Peter got up and went with them. ...they took him to the room upstairs. Peter sent them all out and knelt down and prayed. Then he turned to her body and said, "Tabitha, rise up." She opened her eyes, saw Peter, and sat up. ...and when he had called the holy ones and the widows, he presented her alive."

*Acts 14:8-10 "At Lystra there was a crippled man, lame from birth, when had never walked. He listened to Paul speaking, who looked intently at him, saw that he had the faith to be healed, and called out in a loud voice, "Stand up straight on your feet." He jumped up and began to walk about."*

*Acts 20:9, 10, 12 "…and a young man named Euteychus who was sitting on the window sill was sinking into a deep sleep as Paul talked on and on. Once overcome by sleep, he fell down from the third story and when he was picked up, he was dead. Paul went down, threw himself upon him, and said as he embraced him, "Don't be alarmed; there is life in him." And they took the boy away alive and were immeasurably comforted."*

*Acts 28:3-5 "Paul had gathered a bundle of brushwood and was putting it on the fire when a viper, escaping from the heat, fasted on his hand. When the natives saw the snake hanging from his hand, they said to one another "This man must certainly be a murderer, though he escaped the sea, Justice has not let him remain alive." But he shook the snake off into the fire and suffered no harm."*

## John Louis

*Acts 28:8,9 "It so happened that the father of Publius was sick with a fever and dysentery. Paul visited him and, after praying, laid his hands on him and healed him. After this had taken place, the rest of the sick on the island came to Paul and were cured."*

*Jas 5:13-15 "Is anyone among you suffering? (S)He should pray. Is anyone in good spirits? (S)He should sing praise. Is anyone among you sick? (S)He should summon the presbyters of the church, and they should pray over and anoint with oil in the name of the Lord, and the prayer of the faith will save the sick person, and the Lord will raise (them) up. If he has committed any sins, he will be forgiven."*

*Jas 5:16 "Therefore, confess your sins to one another and pray for one another, that you may be healed. The fervent prayer of a righteous person is very powerful."*

*1Pt 2:1, 2, 5* "*Rid yourselves of all malice and all deceit, insincerity, envy, and all slander; like newborn infants, long for pure spiritual milk so that through it you may grow into salvation…and like living stones, let yourselves be built into a spiritual house to be a holy priesthood to offer spiritual sacrifice acceptable to God through Jesus Christ.*"

# The Nuptial Mass:
# New Life Celebrated With the Body of Christ

The ritual of every sacrament celebrates new life in the Church across the unity of an embodied spirit. The nuptial mass does this with particular significance as "a man leaves his father and mother and clings to his wife, and the two of them become one body" (Gn 2:24). Two spirits, two consciences, two bodies become one living being. This is Gospel in that Jesus quotes this scripture according to Mark Chapter 10 and Matthew Chapter 19. Paul provides more detail on this union in Ephesians Chapter 5 when he describes how husband and wife should relate to each other. These scriptures remain relevant today, where St. Pope John Paul II writes in even greater detail in his work *Man and Woman He Created Them*. "In the Latin Rite the celebration of marriage between two Catholic faithful normally takes place during Holy Mass, because of the connection of all the sacraments with the Paschal mystery of Christ" (CCC #1621).

The process of the two-becoming one begins before the vows are spoken. The human story of boy-meets-girl is a social routine we experience as a natural course of living, learning, and growing. Raised in the Church by diligent parents following their call to be fruitful and multiply, the principles discussed in preceding chapters with the collected scriptures give children the foundation to engage in these relationships. We work, teach, pray, and trust the Spirit to guide our children with the revealed virtues into relationships leading to their commitment to family life and charity.

The Sacrament of Marriage is a life-long covenant relationship between man and woman. It is affirmed by the two, speaking the four-fold vows in public, before God and the witness of the priest, family, and confidants. It is continually renewed daily through the *yes* one gives to the other. This commitment, of wonder, of struggle, of heartache and joy, of discovery, and of wounding and tending of wounds, is the romance of life. It begins in the Church, supported by the Body of Christ called together by the couple.

### *The Church Gathers*
When you, the couple, have called the community together for this celebration, your intention to love each other and profess this love to the community is the reason for drawing together the Body of Christ. This is your public act, to announce a covenant commitment to live in a Christian Marriage and accept all the commitments this includes. It is both a celebration of new life and caution to all others not to interfere. "Therefore, what God has joined no human being must separate" (Mk 10:9). Whatever relationships were explored in the past, whatever interests there might have been, these are put aside for the one, and the public pronouncement makes this known. "Live therefore as children of the light, being filled with the Spirit, conversing among yourselves with psalms, hymns, and spiritual songs, singing and making hymns to the Lord with all your heart" (Eph 5:17 – 19, quoted by JPII, TOB 87).

Know that those you have invited to celebrate this nuptial Mass are processing into heaven with you. In chapters four through eleven of the Book of Revelation, the prayers and praises acclaimed during Mass and your wedding emulate heavenly worship, an intersection in time and space with the Kingdom of God. You are celebrating in time the final verses of chapter 22 of Revelation. "The Spirit and the bride say, 'Come.' Let the hearer say, 'Come'" (Rev 22:17). The prayers and praises of Mass, the design of the church building, and the form of the ritual all stretch back through the scriptural records of how to praise of the Creator. From the meeting tent Moses was instructed to build, to the Temples built by Solomon and Herod, through the apocalyptic visions of Daniel and of John, the church buildings of today are the physical edifices of the living Church you proclaim.

Your individual lives in the Church began with the Sacrament of Baptism, another sacramental ritual initiated by Jesus and affirmed as the beginning of the New Covenant promise in your hearts. We remind ourselves of our Baptism and Confirmation as we enter the church building. We touch the holy water and sign ourselves with the cross to show outwardly that we are part of the committed community. We bless others and ourselves with this visible sign of our faith. St. Pope John Paul the Great reminds us using Paul's letter to the Ephesians, "... Christ loved the Church and gave himself for her, in order to make her holy by cleansing her with the washing of water accompanied by the word, so as to present his Church... all glorious" (Eph 5:21, quoted by JPII TOB #87).

The Bishop/Priest/Deacon presides in the person of Christ, greeting the community, offering peace, with a response recognizing the working of Christ within the presider, "and with your Spirit" (Roman Missal). The first words of Mass affirm we are working in the Spirit of Jesus. Each person present has publicly affirmed their faith as an individual. Next, we ask for healing and affirm our faith as a community.

*Reconciliation*

The priest leads the community in reconciliation. Each person joins with the priest to pray the Confiteor, by asking forgiveness of God and each person present. "I confess to almighty God, and to you my brothers and sisters, that I have greatly sinned," for the transgressions committed since their last confession and each receives grace for their soul, removing inhibitions to listen to God's Word and to share in the Eucharistic celebration. Venial sins are forgiven of all who participate. "May almighty God bless us, forgive us our sins, and bring us to everlasting life." The individual is healed, and the community becomes whole again, one Body "...who wash[ed] their robes so as to have the right to the tree of life and enter the city through its gates" (Rev 22:14).

The Gloria gives praise and worship to one God in the three persons. We praise the Triune God for the benevolent forgiveness and the grace given for continued life. We give our word, initiated from our consciences and then spoken or sung by our persons, that we continue to believe in the Gospel through the Church commissioned by Jesus.

*Liturgy of the Word – God Feeds Our Conscience*
Our introduction included a description of who and what we are in our being, embodied spirit, physical body, and rational mind with the divine gift of conscience. The mind and conscience are fed through our listening and contemplation of the Word and the priest's comments relating the Word to our lives. The readings are chosen by the two of you, reflecting your perspective on the sacrament you called us to witness. Your understanding of the purpose of Mass and making your vows within its context bears on your choice of readings. This is no simple decision of form and format. Your part in planning your wedding scriptures is your first effort at teaching and continuing the life of Christ in the community. Your efforts here begin your act of promise to *be fruitful* as one being. You will make one of your many decisions as *one person* when choosing the readings from scripture for your wedding. You choose to share those passages that best reflect your understanding of the sacrament and your intentions for your sacrament. Through prayer (opening yourself to the Holy Spirit), you, and the counsel of your minister (priest or deacon in persona Christi, and the liturgist) are the teachers of marriage for this gathering of the Church.

You are participating in the greatest bible study program on earth. Your choices bear on both the First Covenant (Old Testament) to prefigure the Eucharist and the New Covenant (New Testament), to fulfill the salvation act, "…the New Testament be hidden in the Old and the Old be made manifest in the New" (Dei Verbum 16). "Do not think that I have come to abolish the law or the prophets. I have come not to abolish but to fulfill" (Mt 5:17). The readings you chose prefigure your joint planning of the life you intend to lead.

## The Celebration of Matrimony; Covenant Vows

"Pietas, fear of God [profound respect for the power of the creator] springing from the profound consciousness of the mystery of Christ, must constitute the basis of the reciprocal relations between the spouses" (St. Pope John Paul II, TOB 87). Your preparation for the Sacrament of Marriage begins in your youth by witnessing the marriage of others, committed as intended here and many, many other examples. It continues as you begin your courtships and test the lessons you learned through witness and study and lessons presented, and how you respond during your courtship together. Engaged, you make a firm decision to consider marriage with your intended. This decision is based on the vows you make to each other. There are four specific promises you will make.

Free Choice - "…have you come here…without coercion, freely and whole heartedly?" (*The Roman Ritual*. The Order of Celebrating Matrimony. USCCB. 2016. Print. p15). You each recognized you are made in the image and likeness of God. As embodied spirits, you exercise free will, decide to make a life-long covenant vow consciously. You recognize you will become one in spirit, mind, and body. There can be no doubt in your willingness to make the choice. You cannot consider anything as a prohibition or impediment to this decision. Pre-marital pregnancy, the insistence of parents and/or guardians (shotgun wedding), economic endeavors or promises (prenuptial contracts) and any other imaginable precondition cannot be part of this decision. These and other considerations may initiate discussions of sacramental marriage. They cannot be, they must *not* be reasons for choosing to marry.

Faithful - "Are you prepared, as you follow the path of Marriage, to love and honor each other… help one another to attain holiness in their married life and in welcoming and educating their children" (*The Roman Ritual*). The marriage bond is three-fold as the embodied spirit is three-fold; spiritually, you commit to common values and principles by which to live. You will approach these from your respective backgrounds. You will strive to present a united commitment to them. Mentally, consciously, you must each determine to act according to the common approach you make. Physically, your actions have simple, common consequences of the mingling of your bodies, from the toothbrush to the meals shared, from the sweetness of a kiss to the engagement in the goods of marriage. Faithfulness preserves the integrity of your union.

Fruitful - Your actions as a unified couple begin the fruitfulness of the marriage. "They look good together" or "They are good together" are phrases adopted in our society, recognizing the value that commitment of a man and woman benefits the two of them as persons. It is a desirable situation. The ultimate goal of marriage is journeying together through life to heaven. The joint activity of daily life becomes the outward sign of covenant commitment to the family and the community through which you live. Your work is recognized as your continuing commitment to the virtues you profess. The power of that commitment will overflow into new creations through projects you promote together and when you join together to create new life.

"Are you prepared to accept children lovingly from God and to bring them up according to the law of Christ and his Church?" (*The Roman Ritual*). The *goods* of marriage focus on procreation as fulfillment of the command of Genesis. Procreation becomes a critical point to test the faithfulness concept discussed. A common approach using the principles of virtue becomes the primary structure for raising and teaching children of their divine gift of living as embodied spirits. Recognition is also given that not all marriages will produce children. The marriage must be open to fertility. The Church clarifies that "new life is not the result of each and every sexual act" (Humanae Vitae #11). The building of a family faithful to the Gospel is part of the intent of the sacrament.

Forever - "…for long as you both shall live" (*The Roman Ritual*). The essence of the journey we are on together through this work is committing to the free-will act is daily, sometimes hourly, as you move through the events of your lives together. This one-time public "I do" becomes a life-long act. It is jointly professed and publicly witnessed, especially by your children, and often by your family and community. This is the nature of a covenant commitment. Your freedom to choose remains and you must repeatedly choose the *other* above all else, seven times seventy-seven. Christ is the source of grace to keep the commitment; you are never alone; though one or the other breaks the covenant, God's grace and presence remain with each, providing an opportunity for reconciliation and renewal of the covenant bond. "For the unbelieving husband is made holy through his wife, and the unbelieving wife is made holy through the brother" (1Cor 7:14). Courtship and the emotions and excitement of the exploration of joined lives rarely leave room for more difficult considerations of life's twists and turns. Covenant love, born of the theological virtues, is the foundation of the forever promise. A community giving prominence to these is the bulwark upon which the torrent seas of social pressures break. 'Forever' is a promise that can be kept. *Forever* is a promise that your joined spirits can make a reality and become the sacramental sign to each other and all your witnesses throughout life.

*You* administer the *sign* of the sacrament, a baptized Christian man and woman, through your exchange of mutual consent (TOB 103:2), by which you swear a covenantal oath to each other. *You* are the outward, visible sign of the invisible spiritual reality of "bone of my bones and flesh of my flesh" (Gen 2:23). A new foundation stone of the living Church is laid by the public pronouncement of this commitment.

Free, faithful, fruitful, and forever is the Sacramental covenant of Marriage. These vows are forged in the crucible of the Commandments, the Virtues, and the Beatitudes. These vows are the embodied spirit being birthed after the gestation of your engagement. Through the waters of Baptism you each walk to the altar and stand before God and His Church, your family, and make the public pronouncement of new life.

*Liturgy of the Eucharist – God feeds our soul and body*
Jesus' instruction to "do this in memory of me" (Lk 22:19) was first practiced in Emmaus on the evening of His resurrection, where "…while he was with them at table, he took bread said the blessing, broke it, and gave it to them. With that their eyes were opened, and they recognized him" (Lk 24:30, 31). The companions didn't know Jesus until the Eucharist was offered. These witnesses, excited and inspired by what they experienced, braved seven miles of dark dirt road, the scrutiny and suspicion of approaching the closed Jerusalem gates, the interrogation of Roman soldiers to enter "the eye of a needle"(Lk 18:25) pedestrian gate (remember, Christians were already under suspicion as rebels), and the darkened streets of Jerusalem to find the Apostles in hiding. All this they did to proclaim his resurrection and how they recognized Him in the breaking of the bread. This is the pinnacle of worship to which you have called the Church together.

We are taught of the Eucharist through the Old Testament and celebrate it throughout the New Testament scriptures. The Old Testament presents the story of Melchizedek, the Priest King of Jerusalem, bringing out bread and wine, blessing the most-high God and his servant Abram (Gn 14). Melchizedek is praised again in Psalm 110. God gives Moses the instructions for the Passover in Egypt, the use of unleavened bread in a meal and the sacrifice of the Passover lamb (Ex 12). Manna is presented to Israel in the desert (Ex 16).

Moses is given instructions on building a meeting tent (Ex 25), directions which still today inform us of how to build our sanctuaries for worship, one in which you have just professed your vows. Jesus is the sacrificial Passover Lamb in the Gospel. In Matthew, Mark, and Luke, he is the Paschal Lamb sacrificed on the cross. John writes to us of the spiritual Lamb, the Bread of Life. Later, in Acts, the story of loaves and fishes on the shores of the lake is told, where Peter is forgiven. St. Paul was the first to write down Christians' actions to fulfill this command. "For I receive from the Lord what I also handed on to you, that the Lord Jesus, on the night he was handed over, took bread, and, after he had given thanks, broke it, and said, 'This is my body that is for you. Do this in remembrance of me'" (1Cor 11:23, 24). It is in the book of Hebrews where Melchizedek is recalled once again to be a precursor of a meal of bread and wine and Jesus' fulfillment of God's covenant.

The Eucharist takes place at the ancient altar of sacrifice. We, the Church, through the example of Revelation, call down the Spirit of God to our table. "Holy, holy, holy…" we sing. Our priest holds his hands over the "works of human hands", the bread and wine, and invokes the Holy Spirit. He repeats the words and actions in persona Christi, and these gifts become the body, blood, soul, and divinity of Christ. We confirm our faith in this divine action; "We proclaim your death, O Lord, and profess your resurrection, until you come again." The priest continues and reminds us that this action has continued, from Apostolic times to today, and we pray for those who lead us, and who have passed on before us. And we affirm all of this with a great "Amen!"

Once again the two of you lead the Church. You affirm your covenant with God by the reception of the Eucharist. You make the public pronouncement together as man and wife of your commitment to the Gospel that this is the body, blood, soul, and divinity of Jesus Christ. Those who believe as you do are offered an opportunity to make their pronouncement as well. The New Testament to the Body of Christ that is the Church is made known to all the witnesses you have invited.

### *The Conclusion of the Celebration – the Church Goes Forth!*

The Nuptial Blessing is offered you as the celebration of Mass comes to a close. It reaffirms the sacramental witness of the Church (the presider and your guests) and calls down the power of the Creator God to bless and strengthen you with His grace. Then, and only then, does the community walk up and accepting the gift of Eucharist, you two-become-one leading the way. The two persons, now one in being, join with the Son of God through the acknowledgment and physical reception of the body, blood, soul, and divinity of Jesus. You have been, as baptized Christians, a part of the Body of Christ. Now, you are a new union, a new proclamation of that same Body, laying down a foundation and continuing to build a free, faithful, and fruitful part of the Body proclaiming the Gospel of Jesus Christ. The Eucharist IS the New Testament, a new testament of faith in God through Jesus Christ. Participation in the Eucharist affirms our commitment as Church to His Divine laws, to the *good news* that is the Gospel we have come to know.

Mass ends as it began. The Priest/Presider invokes God's blessing and grace onto the community of Church you called together for your celebration. The dismissal of the community begins the celebration of the new life that you have become. You invited the community together to be nourished and renewed. You proclaimed new life through your sacramental commitment. You led the community to the Eucharistic table. Now, you lead the community back into the world to proclaim the Gospel through your new life.

# Epilogue

The Western civilization of the twenty-first century has become accustomed to 'drive-through' service, Amazon next-day delivery, and pretty much desire-upon-demand service for material goods to satisfy all our whims as well as needs. The services provided are both welcome as necessary and detrimental in that we no longer have to wait, dream, practice patience, nor suffer deprivation that we use to build and strengthen character. Even divorce, especially divorce, has become an easy acquisition, one that Jesus taught against during His mission (Mk Ch 10; Mt Ch 19)

This is not part of the 'quick-fix' service society. Effort is required. Time must be invested. Will use of this book help you in your efforts? It can. Will use of these exercises and prayer 'fix' your problem? Only you can know that. I can only offer you the following two examples.

Dr. (M.D.) Ed Wheat wrote a simple booklet[2] that set me on my own journey. He chronicled the efforts of two people he knew who wanted to save their marriages when their spouses did not. One woman expressed the peace she was given by her efforts, knowing she was living her marriage vows when her husband would not. He moved on. That is not to say she was sad. Hurt, yes. Carrying a sense of loss? Yes. Sad and distraught? By no means. Her faith in God and her commitment to her covenant vow sustained her and helped her find contentment. It is a rare example of what is presented in both Dr. Wheatly's booklet and this work. It is

---

[2] (Wheatly, Ed. *"How to Save Your Marriage Alone."* Zondervan Press, Grand Rapids; 1983. Print.)

contrary to our culture to even try. But then, Christianity began as counter-culture. Again, read the Gospel accounts in Mark chapter 10 and Matthew 19.

The journey I was set on began with a 'dear john' letter received while I was at sea. A few months along my journey my priest handed me Dr. Wheatly's booklet and said, "Read this. If you still want to save your marriage after, come find me." He was stark. He promised nothing. Neither did Dr. Wheaty. The comprehension of living out my covenant commitment alone became a real possibility. I went and found the priest and he walked the first couple months of the journey with me.

My wife and I remain married and so many years later we are more happily committed than I could have imagined when our trial began. I failed, and often, over the first few years to meet my commitments. Everything you experience in this work and more was part of my own consideration. It took may years of effort before the trust was regained and decisions were jointly made. The analogy of a roller-coaster for the mental and emotional cycles between depression and elation is apt. It was not easy. I cannot promise you anything.

What your journey will bring you is entirely up to you and what you believe and put into practice. I can only tell you it is possible to heal marriage and keep it fruitful or bring it to a place where it will bear fruit again. It will certainly be a different relationship from what it was before the trouble occurred. Nostalgia for the old makes for better understanding of the worth of the new.

I offer you once more the grace and peace of God our Father, the blessings of Jesus our Lord and brother, and the inspiration of the Holy Spirit as you continue on your journey.